Eyewitness
OCEAN

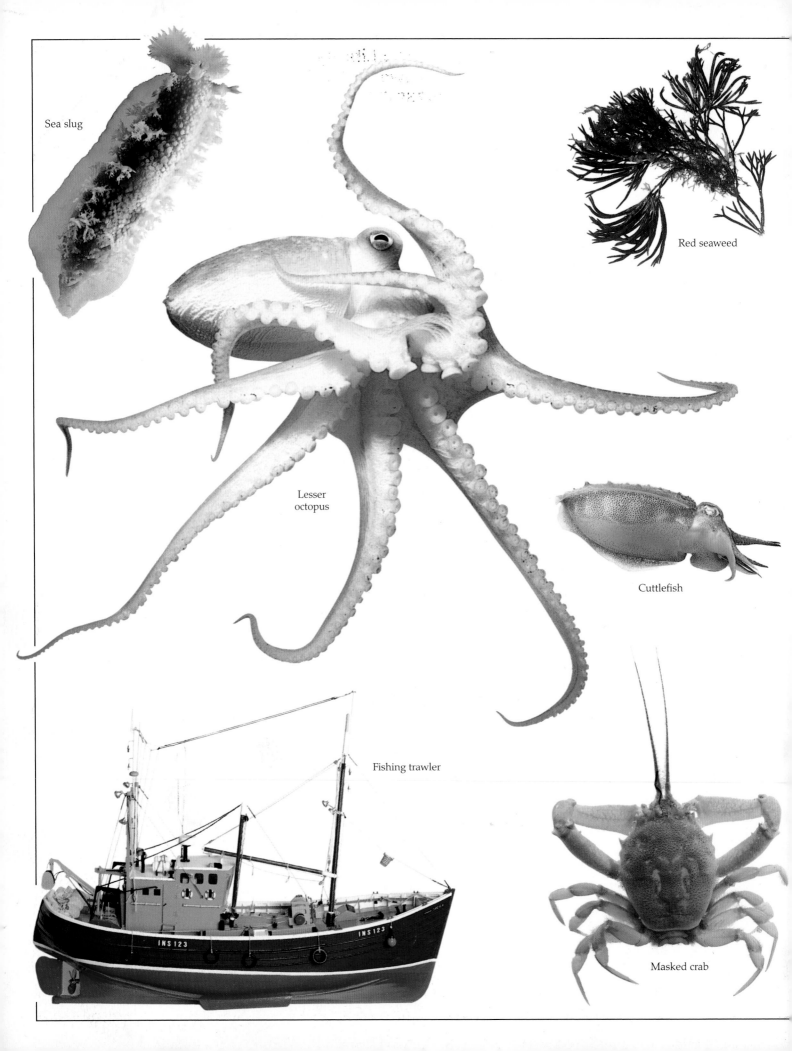

Sea slug

Red seaweed

Lesser
octopus

Cuttlefish

Fishing trawler

INS 123

INS 123

Masked crab

Eyewitness
OCEAN

Boar fish

European
spiny lobster

Written by
DR. MIRANDA MACQUITTY

Photographed by
FRANK GREENAWAY

Butterfly blenny

Maerl
seaweed

Common
sea urchin

DK Publishing

Common starfish

Parchment worm inside its tube

Red cushion star

DK

LONDON, NEW YORK,
MELBOURNE, MUNICH, and DELHI

Project editor Marion Dent
Art editor Jane Tetzlaff
Managing editor Gillian Denton
Managing art editor Julia Harris
Research Céline Carez
Picture research Kathy Lockley
Production Catherine Semark
Special thanks The University Marine Biological
Station (Scotland) and Sea Life Centres (UK)

THIS EDITION
Editors Sue Nicholson,
Victoria Heywood-Dunne, Marianne Petrou
Art editors Andrew Nash, David Ball
Managing editors Andrew Macintyre, Camilla Hallinan
Managing art editors Jane Thomas, Martin Wilson
Publishing manager Sunita Gahir
Production editors Siu Yin Ho, Andy Hilliard
Production controllers Jenny Jacoby, Pip Tinsley
Picture research Deborah Pownall, Sarah Smithies
DK picture library Rose Horridge, Myriam Megharbi, Emma Shepherd
U.S. editorial Elizabeth Hester, Beth Sutinis
U.S design and DTP Dirk Kaufman, Milos Orlovic
U.S. production Chris Avgherinos

This Eyewitness ® Guide has been conceived by
Dorling Kindersley Limited and Editions Gallimard

First published in the United States in 1995
This revised edition published in 2003, 2008 by DK Publishing,
375 Hudson Street, New York, New York 10014

Copyright © 1995, © 2003, © 2008 Dorling Kindersley Limited

11 12 10 9 8
009 – ED633 – Jun/2008

A catalog record for this book is
available from the Library of Congress

ISBN 978-0-7566-3776-7

Color reproduction by Colourscan, Singapore
Printed and bound by Toppan Printing (Shenzhen) Ltd., China

Discover more at

www.dk.com

Mussel shells

Red cushion star

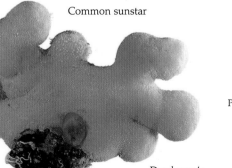

Prepared slides

Common sunstar

Dead man's fingers

Victorian collection of shells

Preserving jar containing a Norwegian lobster

Microscope used in the late 1800s

Contents

Squat lobster

Oceans of the past

THE EARTH, WITH ITS VAST EXPANSES of ocean, has not always looked the way it does today. Over millions of years the land masses have drifted across the face of the planet as new oceans opened up and old oceans have disappeared. Today's oceans only started to take shape in the last 200 million years of the Earth's 4.6-billion-year existence. But water in the form of vapor was present in the atmosphere of the early Earth. As the Earth cooled, water vapor condensed, making storm clouds from which rain fell and eventually filled the oceans. Water also came from space in the form of icy comets. As the oceans themselves changed, so too did life within the oceans. Simple organisms first appeared in the oceans 3.5 million years ago and were followed by more and more complex life forms. Some forms of life became extinct, but others still survive in the ocean today, more or less unchanged.

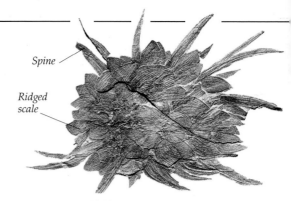

Spine

Ridged scale

TOPSY TURVY WORLD
Wiwaxia lived on the seafloor 530 million years ago, yet this fossil was found high above sea level in Canada's Rocky Mountains. This shows just how much the Earth's surface has changed, with land, originally formed under the sea, forced up to form mountain chains.

Strong belly ribs protected underside of bulky, rounded body

Short tail relative to total body length

Femur, or thigh bone, articulated with pelvic girdle

Arm used for moving and catching food

Huge, long, flat flipper made up of five rows of elongated toes

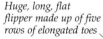

Fossil brittle star, *Palaeocoma*

STILL HERE TODAY
This 180-million-year-old fossil brittle star looks like its living relative (above). Brittle stars have a round central disk and five, very fragile, jointed arms, that can easily break. Today, as in the past, large numbers are often found on sandy or muddy seabeds.

ANCIENT CORAL

Compared to their soft-bodied relatives the anemones and jellyfish, corals were preserved well as fossils in rocks because of their hard skeletons, such as this 400-million-year-old fossil coral. Each coral animal formed a skeleton joining that of its neighbor to create chains with large spaces between them.

CHANGING OCEANS

One giant ocean, Panthalassa, surrounded the supercontinent Pangaea (1), 290–240 mya (million years ago). At the end of this period, many kinds of marine life became extinct. Pangaea broke up, with part drifting north and part south, with the Tethys Sea between.

CONTINENTAL DRIFT

The northern part split to form the North Atlantic 208–146 mya (2). The South Atlantic and Indian Oceans began to form 146–65 mya (3). The continents continued to drift 1.64 mya (4). Today the oceans are still changing shape—the Atlantic Ocean gets wider by an inch or so each year.

Most flexible vertebrae in neck

Long neck and small head typical of one type of plesiosaur

Plated arm in life had feather-like feeding structures

Sharp, interlocking teeth for capturing fish prey

MARINE REPTILES

The first reptiles mostly lived on land, but some of their spectacular descendants became adapted for life in the sea. Among the best known are the plesiosaurs. They first appeared around 200 million years ago. Plesiosaurs swam using their flippers, as either oars or wings—to "fly" through the water like turtles do today. They eventually died out around 65 million years ago along with their land-based cousins, the dinosaurs. The only true ocean-dwelling reptiles today are the sea snakes and sea turtles.

All-around vision provided by large, curved eye

Smaller, front flipper also had five elongated toes

SEA LILY

A complete fossil of a sea lily (crinoid) is quite a rare find even though large numbers of these animals grew on the bottom of ancient oceans. The skeleton, composed of small bony plates, usually broke up when the animal died. Although they are far less numerous today, sea lilies are still found living below 330 ft (100 m). Sea lilies are relatives of feather stars, but unlike them are usually anchored to the seabed. Their arms surround an upward-facing mouth and are used to trap small particles of food drifting by.

Segmented body allowed trilobite to roll up like a woodlouse

Long, flexible stem anchored crinoid in seabed gardens

DEAD AND GONE

Trilobites, one of the most abundant creatures living in the ancient seas, first flourished over 510 million years ago. They had jointed limbs and an external skeleton like insects and crustaceans (such as crabs and lobsters) but they died out some 250 million years ago.

Oceans today

Leafy sea dragon

DIP A TOE IN ANY OCEAN and you are linked to all the world's oceans as the earth's seawater is one continuous mass. The largest expanses are called oceans while the smaller ones (usually close to, or partly enclosed by, land) are called seas. Two-thirds of the Earth's surface is covered by seawater, which makes up to 97 percent of the planet's entire water supply. Seawater's temperature varies in different areas—it is colder at the surface in polar regions than in the tropics. Generally, seawater gets colder with depth. Seawater's salinity varies from that of the saltiest waters (such as the desert-bound Red Sea where there is a high evaporation rate and little inflow of freshwater) to one of the least salty (the Baltic Sea where there is a high inflow of freshwater from rivers). Nor is the bottom of the ocean the same everywhere. There are undersea mountains, plateaus, plains, and trenches, making the ocean floor as complex as any geological formations on land.

Haiti/Dominican Republic

Sea level

Tobago

Trinidad

North coast of Venezuela

South America

Georgetown (capital of Guyana)

Continental shelf

Model (right) of a section of the seafloor east of the Caribbean, as shown in red square on map (below)

Guiana Plateau

Continental slope

PACIFIC OCEAN   Bering Sea   ARCTIC OCEAN   Sargasso Sea

Baltic Sea

Arabian Sea

Mediterranean Sea

INDIAN OCEAN

Coral Sea   Tasman Sea   SOUTHERN OCEAN   Caribbean Sea   ATLANTIC OCEAN

OCEANS OF OCEANS

The world's five oceans, ranging from the largest to the smallest, are the Pacific, Atlantic, Indian, Southern, and Arctic. The Pacific Ocean, by far the largest, covers 59 million sq miles (153 million sq km) and is about 13 times the size of the Arctic Ocean. The Arctic Ocean's center is permanently covered by a layer of sea ice that grows larger in winter and shrinks in summer by melting. Over half the Southern Ocean is also frozen in winter and sea ice still fringes the continent of Antarctica during the summer. The average depth of all the oceans is 12,000 ft (3,650 m) with the deepest part in the Pacific Ocean at 36,201 ft (11,034 m) in the Mariana Trench, east of the Philippines.

SEA OR LAKE?
The water in the Dead Sea is saltier than any ocean because the water that drains into it evaporates in the hot sun, leaving behind the salts. A body is more buoyant in such salty water, making it easier to float. The Dead Sea is a lake, not a sea, because it is completely surrounded by land. True seas are always connected to the ocean by a channel.

Floating on the
Dead Sea

GOD OF THE WATERS
Neptune, the Roman god of the sea, is usually shown riding a dolphin and carrying a pronged spear (trident). It was thought he also controlled freshwater supplies, so offerings were made to him at the driest time of the year.

DISAPPEARING ACT
The gigantic plates on the Earth's crust move like a conveyor belt. As new areas of ocean floor form at spreading centers, old areas disappear into the molten heart of the planet. This diagram shows one oceanic plate being forced under another (subduction) in the Mariana Trench, creating an island arc.

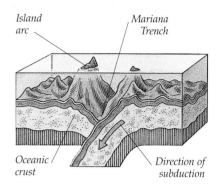

Island arc *Mariana Trench*

Oceanic crust *Direction of subduction*

Formation of Mariana Trench

Hatteras Abyssal Plain

Puerto Rico Trench

Nares Abyssal Plain

Mid-Atlantic Ridge

Kane Fracture Zone

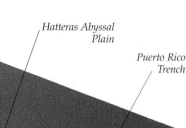

Vema Fracture Zone

Demerara Abyssal Plain

THE OCEAN FLOOR
This model shows the features on the bottom of the Atlantic Ocean off the northeast coast of South America from Guyana to Venezuela. Off this coast is the continental shelf, a region of relatively shallow water about 660 ft (200 m) deep. Here the continental shelf is about 125 miles (200 km) wide, but off the coast of northern Asia it is as much as 1,000 miles (1,600 km) wide. At the outer edge of the continental shelf, the ocean floor drops away steeply to form the continental slope. Sediments eroded from the land and carried by rivers, such as the Orinoco, accumulate at the bottom of this continental slope. The ocean floor then opens out in virtually flat areas (abyssal plains), which are covered with a deep layer of soft sediments. The Puerto Rican Trench formed where one of the Earth's plates (the North American Plate) is sliding past another (the Caribbean Plate). An arc of volcanic islands has also been created where the North American Plate is forced under the Caribbean Plate. The fracture zones are offsets of the Mid-Atlantic Ridge.

Life in the oceans

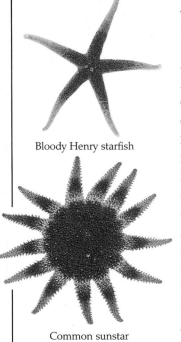

Bloody Henry starfish

Common sunstar

FROM THE SEA SHORE to the deepest depths, oceans are home to some of the most diverse life on Earth. Animals live either on the seabed or in midwater where they swim or float. Plants are only found in the sunlit zone where there is enough light for them to grow either anchored to the bottom or drifting in the water. Animals are found at all depths of the oceans, but are most abundant in the sunlit zone where food is plentiful. Not all free-swimming animals stay in one zone—the sperm whale dives to over 1,650 ft (500 m) to feed on squid, returning to the surface to breathe air. Some animals from cold, deep waters, such as the Greenland shark in the Atlantic, are also found in the cold, surface waters of polar regions. Over 90 percent of all species dwell on the bottom. One rock can be home to at least 10 major types, such as corals, mollusks, and sponges. Most ocean animals and plants have their origins in the sea, but some like whales and sea grasses are descended from ancestors that once lived on land.

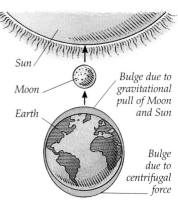

Sun
Moon
Earth

Bulge due to gravitational pull of Moon and Sun

Bulge due to centrifugal force

TIME AND TIDE
Anyone spending time by the seaside or in an estuary will notice the tides. Tides are caused by the gravitational pull of the Moon on the Earth's mass of seawater. An equal and opposite bulge of water occurs on the side of the Earth away from the Moon, due to centrifugal force. As the Earth spins on its axis, the bulges (high tides) usually occur twice a day in any one place. The highest and lowest tides occur when the Moon and Sun are in line causing the greatest gravitational pull. These are the spring tides at new and full Moon.

SHORE LIFE
Often found on the shore at low tide, starfish also live in deeper water. Sea life on the shore must either be tough enough to withstand drying out, or shelter in rock pools. The toughest animals and plants live high on the shore, but the least able to cope in air are found at the bottom.

SQUISHY SQUID
Squid are among the most common animals living in the ocean. Like fish, they often swim around in shoals for protection in numbers. Their torpedo-shaped bodies are streamlined so they can swim fast.

Inside squid's soft body is a horny, penlike shell

Funnel expels jet of water for moving in the sea

Tentacles reach out to grasp food

Continental shelf

Flying fish

Man-of-war

Shark

Oarweed

Mackerel

Turtle

Brain coral

Continental slope

Sperm whale

Sponges

Octopus

Hatchet fish

Sea pens

Rat-tail fishes

Gulper eel

Sea spider

Anglerfish

Abyssal plain

Sea cucumbers

Brittle star

Flower-basket sponge

Tripod fish

Deep-sea anemone

Note: Neither the marine life nor zones are drawn to scale

Sunlit zone
0–650 ft
(0–200 m)

Twilight zone
650–3,300 ft
(200–1,000 m)

Dark zone
3,300–13,000 ft
(1,000–4,000 m)

Abyss
13,000–20,000 ft
(4,000–6,000 m)

Trench
Over 20,000 ft
(6,000 m)

Deep-sea cat shark grows to only 20 in (50 cm) long

THE OCEAN'S ZONES
The ocean is divided up into broad zones, according to how far down sunlight penetrates, and water temperature and pressure. In the sunlit zone, there is plenty of light, much water movement, and seasonal changes in temperature. Beneath this is the twilight zone, the maximum depth where light penetrates. Temperatures here decrease rapidly with depth to about 41°F (5°C). Deeper yet is the dark zone, where there is no light and temperatures drop to about 34–36°F (1–2°C). Still in darkness and even deeper is the abyss and then the trenches. There are also zones on the seabed. The shallowest zone lies on the continental shelf. Below this are the continental slope, the abyssal plains, and the seafloor trenches.

GIANT AMONG SEA FIRS

Standing about 3 ft (1 m) tall above the seabed, this giant sea fir was first discovered in the 1875 voyage of HMS *Challenger* when a specimen was trawled up from the ocean floor off the Japanese coast. In 1985, the first observations on living specimens were made from the Japanese submersible, *Shinkai 2000*. The sea fir catches food drifting by in its long tentacles and can even tackle tiny fish, up to 1 in (2 cm) long. Specimens have been found in the Pacific Ocean at depths from 165 to 17,500 ft (50 to 5,300 m), as well as in the Atlantic Ocean. Unlike other sea firs (pp. 20–21), the giant sea fir is a solitary individual, not a branching colony.

Stinging tentacles surround mouth

Floating fronds can grow to 150 ft (45 m) long, forming a floating canopy on water's surface

MAGNIFICENT WEED

Growing up from the bottom, the giant kelp has a central, stemlike stalk, covered with leaflike blades. At its base, each blade has a gas-filled air bladder, which keeps the kelp afloat. By spreading out its blades, the kelp absorbs the maximum amount of sunshine for making food by photosynthesis. Giant kelps are among the fastest growing plants in the world, growing over 1 ft (0.3 m) a day. Off North America's Pacific coast, kelp forests provide a home for such animals as sea otters and sea urchins. They are also harvested for jellylike alginate, used to make ice cream and other products.

Long tentacles catch food drifting by in sea

Model of the largest-known giant sea fir (Branchiocerianthus imperator)

First dorsal fin is placed well back on shark's body

Sea fir's stem grows out of muddy sand

Large pectoral fin

DEEP-SEA SHARK

Most people think of sharks as dangerous predators, but cat sharks are quite harmless. This one is from the deep Pacific Ocean. Sharks living in deep water do not have problems with buoyancy, because unlike some bony fishes they do not have gas-filled air bladders. Instead, all sharks have oil-rich livers, which help reduce their weight in water.

Very long caudal (tail) fin

ICY OCEAN

There are two main types of sea ice—pack ice that forms on the surface of the open sea (as here in Canada's Hudson Bay) and fast ice that forms between the land and the pack ice. Because of its salt content, seawater freezes at lower temperatures than freshwater. Since cold water sinks and is replaced by warmer water, it takes a long time before the water is cold enough for ice to form. Icebergs are huge chunks broken off the polar ice sheets and glaciers, formed from freshwater on land.

Waves and weather

SEAWATER IS CONSTANTLY moving. At the surface, wind-driven waves can be 50 ft (15 m) from crest to trough. Major surface currents are driven by the prevailing winds. Both surface and deep-water currents help modify the world's climate by taking cold water from the polar regions toward the tropics, and vice versa. Shifts in this flow affect life in the ocean. In an El Niño climatic event, warm water starts to flow down the west of South America, which stops nutrient-rich, cold water rising up, causing plankton growth to slow and fisheries to fail. Heat from oceans creates air movement, from swirling hurricanes to daytime breezes on-shore, or nighttime ones off-shore. Breezes occur as the ocean heats up more slowly than the land in the day. Cool air above the water blows in, replacing warm air above the land, and the reverse at night.

DOWN THE SPOUT
Water spouts (spinning sprays sucked up from the surface) begin when whirling air drops down from a storm cloud to the ocean.

RIVERS OF THE SEA
Currents are huge masses of water moving through the oceans. The course currents follow is not precisely the same as the trade winds and westerlies, because currents are deflected by land and the Coriolis Force produced by the Earth's rotation. The latter causes currents to shift to the right in the northern hemisphere and to the left in the southern. There are also currents that flow due to differences in density of seawater.

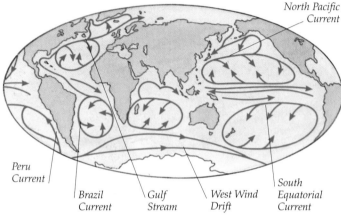

North Pacific Current

Peru Current

Brazil Current

Gulf Stream

West Wind Drift

South Equatorial Current

Day 2: Thunderstorms as swirling cloud mass

Day 4: Winds have increased in intensity

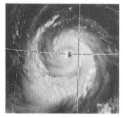

Day 7: Strong winds

A HURRICANE IS BORN
These satellite photographs show a hurricane developing. On day 2 a swirling cloud mass is formed. By day 4 fierce winds develop about the center. By day 7 winds are the strongest.

Ice forms at the very top of the clouds

Hurricanes are enormous—some may be 500 miles (800 km) across

Warm, moist air spirals up around the eye inside the hurricane

Torrential rains fall from clouds

Energy to drive storm comes from warm ocean at 80°F (27°C) or more

Strongest winds of up to 220 mph (360 kph) occur just outside the eye

HEART OF A HURRICANE
Hurricanes (also known as typhoons) are the most destructive forces created by the oceans. They develop in the tropics where warm, moist air rises up from the ocean's surface creating storm clouds. As more air spirals upward, energy is released, fueling stronger winds that whirl around the eye (a calm area of extreme low pressure). Hurricanes move onto land and cause terrible devastation. Away from the ocean, hurricanes die out.

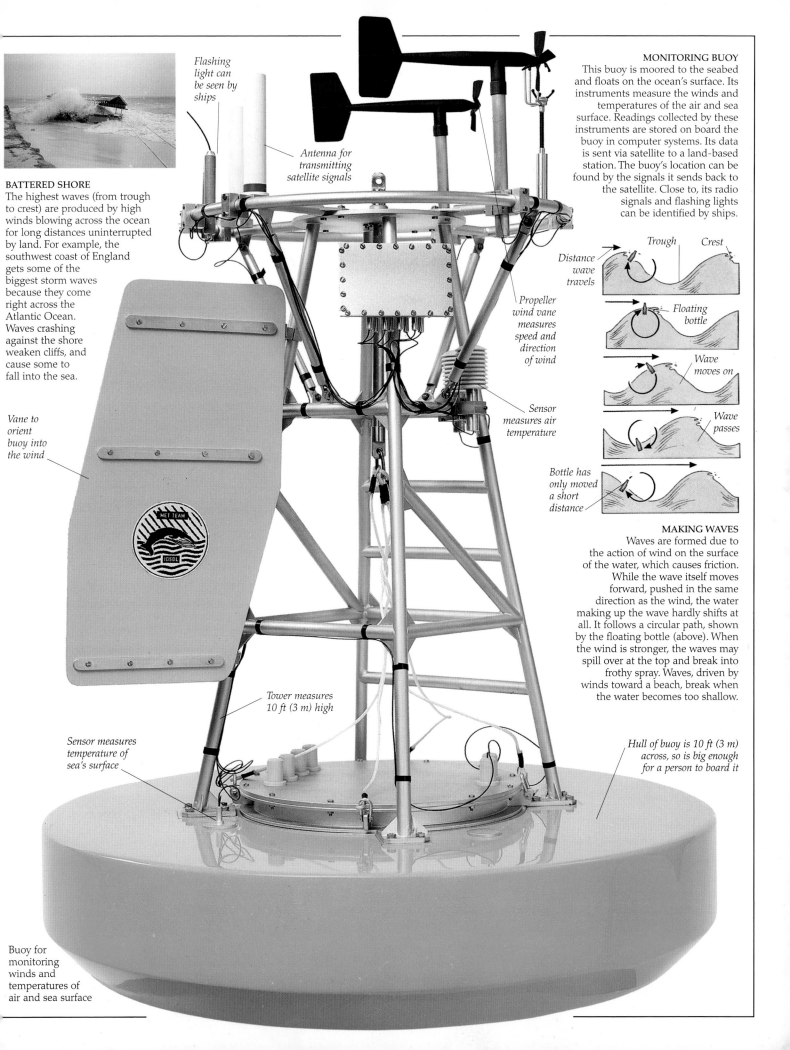

Flashing light can be seen by ships

Antenna for transmitting satellite signals

MONITORING BUOY
This buoy is moored to the seabed and floats on the ocean's surface. Its instruments measure the winds and temperatures of the air and sea surface. Readings collected by these instruments are stored on board the buoy in computer systems. Its data is sent via satellite to a land-based station. The buoy's location can be found by the signals it sends back to the satellite. Close to, its radio signals and flashing lights can be identified by ships.

BATTERED SHORE
The highest waves (from trough to crest) are produced by high winds blowing across the ocean for long distances uninterrupted by land. For example, the southwest coast of England gets some of the biggest storm waves because they come right across the Atlantic Ocean. Waves crashing against the shore weaken cliffs, and cause some to fall into the sea.

Vane to orient buoy into the wind

Propeller wind vane measures speed and direction of wind

Sensor measures air temperature

Trough *Crest*

Distance wave travels

Floating bottle

Wave moves on

Wave passes

Bottle has only moved a short distance

MAKING WAVES
Waves are formed due to the action of wind on the surface of the water, which causes friction. While the wave itself moves forward, pushed in the same direction as the wind, the water making up the wave hardly shifts at all. It follows a circular path, shown by the floating bottle (above). When the wind is stronger, the waves may spill over at the top and break into frothy spray. Waves, driven by winds toward a beach, break when the water becomes too shallow.

Tower measures 10 ft (3 m) high

Sensor measures temperature of sea's surface

Hull of buoy is 10 ft (3 m) across, so is big enough for a person to board it

Buoy for monitoring winds and temperatures of air and sea surface

Sandy and muddy

IN SHALLOW COASTAL WATERS, from the lowest part of the shore to the edge of the continental shelf, sand and mud are washed from the land, creating vast stretches of seafloor which look like underwater deserts. Finer-grained mud settles in places where the water is calmer. Without rocks, there are no abundant growths of seaweeds, so animals that venture onto the surface are exposed to predators. Many of the creatures avoid them by hiding in the soft seabed. Some worms hide inside their own tubes, but they can feed by spreading out a fan of tentacles or by drawing water containing food particles into their tubes. Other worms, such as the sea mouse, move around in search of food. Flat fish, like the flounder, are commonly found on the sandy seabed, looking for any readily available food, such as peacock worms. All the animals shown here live in the coastal waters of the Atlantic Ocean.

Tough papery tube protects soft worm inside

Worm can grow up to 16 in (40 cm) long

Bulky body covered by dense mat of fine hairs

Coarse, shiny bristles help it to move along seabed

BEAUTIFUL BRISTLE WORM
The sea mouse plows its way through muddy sand on the seabed and is often washed up on the beach after storms. The shiny, rainbow-colored spines help propel it along and may make this chunky worm less appetizing to fish. The sea mouse usually keeps its rear end out of the sand to bring in a stream of fresh sea water to help it breathe. Sea mice grow to 4 in (10 cm) long and eat any dead animals they may find in the sand.

Light color helps it merge into sand

Thick trunk looks like a peanut, when whole body retracts

Surface of plump, unsegmented body feels rough

Poisonous spines on first dorsal fin

PEANUT WORM
Many different groups of worms live in the sea. This is one of the sipunculid worms, sometimes called peanut worms. A stretchy front part can retract into the thicker trunk. Peanut worms usually burrow in sand and mud, but some of these 320 different kinds of worm live in empty sea shells and in coral crevices.

Front part can also retract

Poisonous spine on front of gill cover

High-set eye allows all-around vision

Mouth surrounded by tentacles

WARY WEEVER
When a weever fish is buried in sand, its eyes on top of its head help it see what is going on. The weever's strategically placed poisonous spines provide it with extra defence. The spines can inflict nasty wounds on humans, if a weever is accidentally trodden on in shallow water or caught in fishermen's nets.

FLAT FISH
Flounders cruise along the seabed looking for food. They can nibble the tops off peacock worms, if they are quick enough to catch them.

Feelerlike palps (sense organs)

Fan-shaped flaps beat to let food pass along worm's body

Parapodia, or feetlike flaps

Parapodia

Red seaweed grows on whitish ends of tube

Tentacle, extended in water, used for feeding and breathing

Mouth

Parchment worm outside its tube

Fan-shaped flap

When buried, the tube is often U-shaped

Parapodia

A LOOK INSIDE
This bizarre looking worm lives in a U-shaped tube with ends that stick out above the mud's surface. The worm feeds by drawing water containing food into its tube. Fan-shaped flaps in the middle of the worm's body create a water current. Food is trapped in a slimy net that is rolled up and passed toward the mouth. A new net is then made and the process repeated. At night this worm can eject a cloud of glowing material from its burrow, perhaps to ward off predators.

Tentacles disappear fast into tube, if danger is present

LIKE A PEACOCK'S FAN
With their crown of tentacles, peacock worms look like plants, not animals. To help them feed and breathe, tiny hairs on the tentacles' fine fringes create a water current that passes through the crown. Particles in this current are passed down rows of beating hairs into the mouth in the crown's center. Larger particles, such as sand grains, are not eaten but help make the tube instead.

Peacock worm can be 10 in (25 cm) long

Tube made of mud and sand bound together with worm's hardened slime

Soft seabed

SWIMMING OVER a soft seabed, using a mask and snorkel, it is possible to see only a few animals because most of them live buried in the sand. Look closely and you may see signs of buried life (a crab's feathery antennae or a clam's siphon), which help these animals get a clean supply of water containing oxygen to breathe. Some fish, like the eagle ray, visit the soft seabed to feed on burrowing clams. Other animals are found only where sea grasses grow on sandy bottoms. Sea grasses are not seaweeds but flowering plants. They are food for many animals, including dugongs and manatees—the only plant-eating marine mammals.

Tough skin protects dugong

DOCILE DUGONG
Dugongs live in shallow tropical waters where they feed on sea grasses growing in the soft seabed. They often dig down into the sand to eat the food-rich roots of sea grasses. These gentle, shy animals are still hunted in some places.

SHELL BOAT
In Botticelli's *The Birth of Venus*, the Roman goddess rises from the water in a scallop shell. In real life, scallop shells are too heavy to float and much too small to carry a person.

Anemonelike polyp unfurls when feeding

ELEGANT PEN
Looking like an old-fashioned quill pen, this relative of sea anemones lives in the soft seabed. The rows of tiny polyps which come out on each side of its body are used to capture small animals drifting by for food. Sea pens glow in the dark if disturbed. Some sea pens grow on the bottom of the deep ocean.

This sea pen can grow to 8 in (20 cm) in height

Long dorsal fin runs along almost whole length of body

RED BAND FISH
This fish usually lives in burrows in the soft seabed, down to depths of about 650 ft (200 m). It is also found swimming among sea grasses. Sometimes red band fish are found washed up on the beach after storms. When out of its burrow, the fish swims by passing waves down its body. It feeds on small animals drifting by.

Long anal fin

Red band fish may grow to 28 in (70 cm) in length

Stem of sea pen anchors in sandy seabed

Tube-feet for breathing

Tube-feet get rid of waste matter

Foot helps clam burrow

Tube-foot pushes food toward mouth

BREATHING IN A BURROW
The sand gaper clam (left) has two tubelike siphons. One takes in water, passing it over the gills where food and oxygen are taken up, then water leaves through the second siphon. The sea potato (above right) breathes with its long tube-feet reaching up to the sand's surface.

Front claw, or pincers

MASKED CRAB
If dug out of the sand, this crab quickly buries itself again. Usually it hides in sand during the day with only its two antennae sticking out. These feelers have bristles linking them together to form a breathing tube when the crab is buried. Water passes down the breathing tube over the crab's gills. At night, the crab comes out of the sand to find food such as small shrimp.

Facelike markings on shell give crab its name

Back leg used for digging

Antennae linked together by bristles

Seahorse can be up to 5 in (12 cm) long

Dorsal fin beats 20 to 35 times per second

Horselike head

Seahorse uncurls tail to rise up in water

HANDY TAIL
Seahorses do not like living in the open, so are found usually among corals, seagrasses, or seaweeds. They are able to hang onto animals or plants with their tails. Unlike most fish, seahorses swim with their bodies upright in the water and move by waves passing down their dorsal fin. They eat small animals that they suck into their delicate mouths.

Tail curls round sea-weed for anchorage

Large eye helps to spot prey

Short pectoral fin

Pectoral fin, or wing, beats up and down when ray swims, looking as if it is "flying"

Eagle ray can grow to 80 in (200 cm) long

A "FLYING" RAY
The eagle ray feeds on the seabed, searching out shellfish with its snout. The shellfish are crushed between bands of flattened teeth. A ray cousin, the spotted eagle ray, can dip its winglike pectoral fins into mud to pull out clams by using suction.

Bulgy, fleshy head

Pointed snout

Rocks underwater

Rocks make up the seabed in coastal waters, where currents sweep away any sand and mud. With the strong water movement, animals must cling onto rocks, find crevices to hide in, or shelter in seaweeds. A few remarkable animals, such as the piddocks (clams) and some sea urchins, can bore into solid rock to make their homes. Sea urchins bore cavities in hard rock while piddocks drill into softer rocks such as sandstone and chalk. Some animals hide under small stones, but only if they are lodged in the soft seabed. Where masses of loose pebbles roll around, animals and seaweeds can be crushed. However, some crustaceans, such as lobsters, can regrow a lost limb crushed by a stone and starfish can regrow a missing arm. Some animals can survive on the seashore's lower levels, especially rock pools, but many need to be continually submerged.

Sea urchin boring into rocks

Piddock

ROCK BORERS
Some sea urchins use their spines and teeth beneath their shells to bore spaces in rock, while piddocks drill with the tips of their shells. Using its muscular foot, the piddock twists and turns to drill and hold onto its burrow. Both are found in shallow water and on the lower shore.

BEAUTIFUL BUTTERFLY
Blennies, small fishes living in shallow water, often rest on the bottom and hide in crannies. They lay their eggs in sheltered places, such as abandoned bottles, and guard them from predators. Blennies feed on small creatures, such as mites, and live on rocky or stony ground to depths of 65 ft (20 m).

Dorsal fin has eyespot to frighten predators

Spiny shell helps deter predators

SPINY LOBSTER
European spiny lobsters, or crawfish, are reddish-brown in life. With their small pincers, spiny lobsters are restricted to eating soft prey such as worms, or devouring dead animals. They live among rocks, hiding in crevices during the day, but venture out over the seabed to find food at night. Some kinds of spiny lobsters move in long lines keeping touch with the lobster in front with their antennae.

Delicate claw on tip of walking leg

European spiny lobster also known as a crayfish or crawfish

Leg used for walking

Tail can be flapped so lobster can swim backward

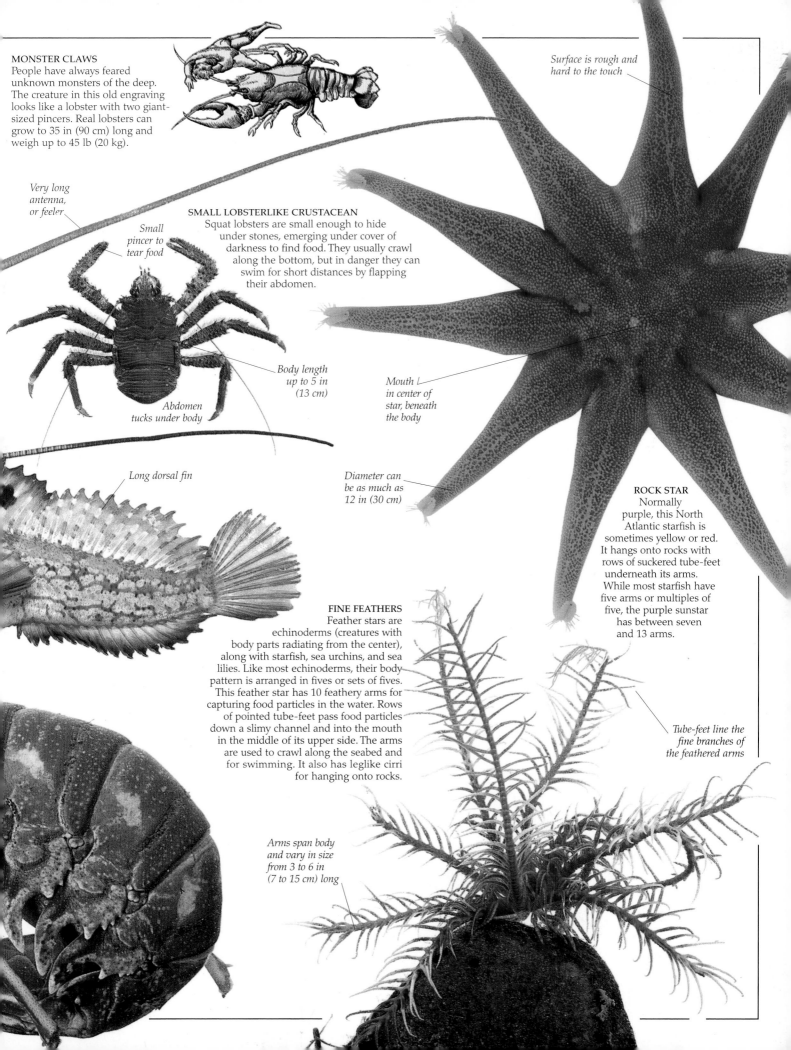

MONSTER CLAWS
People have always feared unknown monsters of the deep. The creature in this old engraving looks like a lobster with two giant-sized pincers. Real lobsters can grow to 35 in (90 cm) long and weigh up to 45 lb (20 kg).

Surface is rough and hard to the touch

Very long antenna, or feeler

Small pincer to tear food

SMALL LOBSTERLIKE CRUSTACEAN
Squat lobsters are small enough to hide under stones, emerging under cover of darkness to find food. They usually crawl along the bottom, but in danger they can swim for short distances by flapping their abdomen.

Body length up to 5 in (13 cm)

Abdomen tucks under body

Mouth in center of star, beneath the body

Long dorsal fin

Diameter can be as much as 12 in (30 cm)

ROCK STAR
Normally purple, this North Atlantic starfish is sometimes yellow or red. It hangs onto rocks with rows of suckered tube-feet underneath its arms. While most starfish have five arms or multiples of five, the purple sunstar has between seven and 13 arms.

FINE FEATHERS
Feather stars are echinoderms (creatures with body parts radiating from the center), along with starfish, sea urchins, and sea lilies. Like most echinoderms, their body pattern is arranged in fives or sets of fives. This feather star has 10 feathery arms for capturing food particles in the water. Rows of pointed tube-feet pass food particles down a slimy channel and into the mouth in the middle of its upper side. The arms are used to crawl along the seabed and for swimming. It also has leglike cirri for hanging onto rocks.

Tube-feet line the fine branches of the feathered arms

Arms span body and vary in size from 3 to 6 in (7 to 15 cm) long

On the rocks

IN SHALLOW, COOL WATERS above rocky seabeds, forests of kelp (large brown seaweeds) are home for many animals. Fish swim among the giant fronds. Along North America's Pacific coast, sea otters wrap themselves in kelp while asleep on the surface. Tightly gripping the rocks, the kelp's rootlike anchor (holdfast) houses hordes of tiny creatures, such as worms and mites. Unlike the roots of land plants, kelp's holdfast is only an anchor and does not absorb water or nutrients. Other animals grow on the kelp's surface or directly on the rocks and capture food brought to them in the currents. Sea firs look like plants, but are animals belonging to the same group as sea anemones, jellyfish, and corals, and all have stinging tentacles. Anchored to rocks, mussels provide homes for some animals between or within their shells.

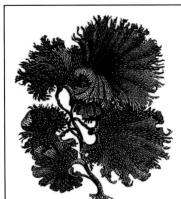

A type of brown seaweed (kelp) found in the Pacific Ocean

DELIGHTFUL MARINE MAMMAL
Sea otters swim and rest among giant kelp fronds along North America's Pacific coast. They dive down to the seabed to pick up shellfish, smashing them open by banging them against a rock balanced on their chest.

ANCHORED ALGAE
Holdfasts of the large, tough, brown algae called kelp keep it firmly anchored to the rocks. Growing in shallow water, kelp is often battered by waves.

Holdfast of oarweed kelp

Holdfast must be strong, as some kinds of kelp can grow tens of metres long

Scaleless body is covered with small warty bumps

PRETTY BABY
Young lumpsuckers are more beautiful than their dumpy parents, which cling onto rocks with suckerlike fins on their bellies. The adult lumpsuckers come into shallow water to breed and the father guards the eggs.

Juvenile lumpsucker

Each sturdy, blunt finger measures at just over an inch (3 cm) across

Fleshy fingers supported by many, tiny, hard splinters

White, anemonelike polyp captures food from fastmoving currents

DEAD MAN'S FINGERS
When this soft coral is washed up on the shore, its rubbery, fleshy form lives up to its name! Growing on rocks, the colonies consist of many polyps (feeding bodies) within a fleshy, orange, or white base.

Gills

SEA MAT
The lacy-looking growth on the kelp's surface (left) is a bryozoan, or moss animal. They live in colonies where many individuals grow next to each other. Each little compartment houses one of these animals, which come out to feed, capturing food in their tiny tentacles. The colony grows as individuals bud off new individuals. Other kinds of moss animal grow upward, looking like seaweeds or corals. Between the sea mats, a blue-rayed limpet grazes on the kelp's surface.

SEA SLUG
Many sea slugs are meat-eaters. This slug lives on the soft coral known as Dead man's fingers. Some sea slugs are able to eat the stinging tentacles of anemones and keep the stings for their own protection. Sea slug eggs hatch into swimming young, which then settle and turn into adults.

LONG LEGS

Spider crabs all have long legs and look like spiders. They hide under rocks and among seaweeds on the lower shore and in shallow waters. Spider crabs make a camouflage by plucking bits of seaweed with their pincers, then attaching these bits to their shells. They crawl over seaweeds hanging on with their claws. Spider crabs can also live on soft seabeds.

Pea crab may nibble mussel's gills

Seaweeds growing on mussel shell

HORSE MUSSEL AND FRIENDS

Heavy-shelled horse mussels live anchored to rocks or kelp holdfasts in shallow water, attached by tough threads. Young mussels settle where another mussel is growing, so gradually a mussel layer builds up on the seabed. Other creatures live among mussels, but the pea crab takes things a stage further. It makes its home within the shell, feeding on the mussel's food.

Seaweed on legs as part of camouflage

Sharp-tipped claw for hanging onto seaweed

Horse mussel grows to 8 in (20 cm) long

Feathery tentacles held on tough, single stems

Anemonelike polyp with two rings of tentacles to capture food

SEA FLOWERS

The beautiful flowerlike polyps of this sea fir (hydroid) are used to capture food. If disturbed, the sea fir will withdraw its polyps into its horny skeleton. Sea firs grow fixed to surfaces, such as rocks and seaweeds, putting out branched colonies of anemonelike polyps. Some sea firs reproduce by budding off tiny jellyfish forms, which shed sperm and eggs into the water. The young sea fir then settles on the bottom. This sea fir (right) does not produce such free-floating shapes. Instead, the jellyfish forms stay attached to the parent sea fir which then releases its young.

Sea mat growing on surface

The coral kingdom

IN THE CRYSTAL CLEAR, WARM WATERS of the tropics, coral reefs flourish, covering vast areas. Made of the skeletons of stony corals, coral reefs are cemented together by chalky algae. Most stony corals are colonies of many tiny, anemonelike individuals, called polyps. Each polyp makes its own hard limestone cup (skeleton) which protects its soft body. To make their skeletons, the coral polyps need the help of microscopic, single-celled algae that live inside them. The algae need sunlight to grow, which is why coral reefs are found only in sunny, surface waters. In return for giving the algae a home, corals get some food from them but also capture plankton with their tentacles. Only the upper layer of a reef is made of living corals, which build upon skeletons of dead polyps. Coral reefs are also home to soft corals and sea fans, which do not have stony skeletons. Related to sea anemones and jellyfish, corals grow in an exquisite variety of shapes (mushroom, daisy, staghorn) and some have colorful skeletons.

Tentacle's stings catch food

Hard plates of stony skeleton

Mouth also expels waste

Baglike stomach

INSIDE A CORAL ANIMAL
In a hard coral, a layer of tissue joins each polyps to its neighbor. To reproduce, they divide in two or release eggs and sperm into the water.

Black coral's horny skeleton looks like a bunch of twigs

Orange sea fan from the Indian and Pacific Oceans

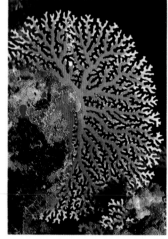

STINGING CORAL
Colorful hydrocorals are related to sea firs and, unlike horny and stony corals, produce jellyfishlike forms that carry their sex organs. Known as fire corals, they have potent stings on their polyps.

BLACK CORAL
In living black corals, the skeleton provides support for the living tissues and the branches bear rows of anemonelike polyps. Black corals are mainly found in tropical waters, growing in the deep part of coral reefs. Although they take a long time to grow, the black skeleton is sometimes used to make jewelry.

Intricate mesh developed to withstand strong currents

Stem of sea fan

SEA FAN

Sea fans are gorgonian corals that have soft tissues growing around a central horny or chalky skeleton. They are more closely related to sea pens, organ-pipe coral, and soft corals than to true stony corals. Most kinds live in tropical waters where they often grow on coral reefs. Some sea fans form branching, treelike shapes (left), but in others the branches join together to form a broad, fan-shaped network. From this structure the anemonelike polyps emerge to strain food from the water's currents.

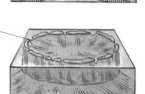

Fringing reef grows around volcano

As volcano subsides lagoon appears, creating barrier reef

Volcano disappears, leaving behind coral atoll

ATOLL IN THE MAKING

An atoll is a ring of coral islands formed around a central lagoon. Charles Darwin (1809–82) thought atolls were formed by a reef growing around a volcanic island which then subsided beneath the surface, a theory later proved to be correct.

Brittle skeleton of organ-pipe coral breaks easily

Branching treelike skeleton

Queen scallops often make their home within the rose coral's folds

Living rose coral (not a true coral) can reach 20 in (50 cm) in diameter

Brain coral gets its name from its convoluted surface that looks like a human brain

ORGAN PIPES

Dull green-colored tissue covers the bright red skeleton of living organ-pipe coral. Its anemonelike polyps emerge from each of the tiny pipes in the skeleton. Organ-pipe coral is not a true stony coral, but a relative of sea fans, soft coral, and sea pens.

A CORAL BY ANY OTHER NAME

Rose coral is moss animal and grows in colonies on the seabed. Each colony is made of millions of tiny animals, each living in one unit in its leaflike structure.

STONE BRAIN

Living brain coral's surface is covered with soft tissue. Anemonelike polyps grow in rows along the channels in its skeleton. Brain corals are slow-growing stony corals, increasing in width just over an inch each year.

BIGGEST AND BEST

Here Australia's Great Barrier Reef shows fish feeding on plankton. Over 1,200 miles (2,000 km) long, it is the largest structure in the world made by living organisms. Of the 400 kinds of coral, many spawn on the same night after a full Moon, the water resembling an underwater snowstorm.

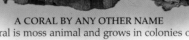

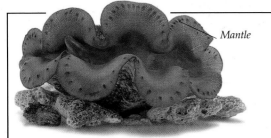

A GIANT CLAM
The giant blue clam grows to about 1 ft (30 cm) long, but the largest giant clams may reach over 3 ft (1 m). The colorful mantle exposed at the edge of their shells contains hordes of single-celled algae that make their own food by using the energy from sunlight. The clam absorbs nutrients from the growing crop of algae.

Mantle

Life on a coral reef

CORAL REEFS HAVE an amazing variety of marine life, from teeming multitudes of brightly colored fish to giant clams wedged into rocks. Every bit of space on the reef provides a hiding place or shelter for some animal or plant. At night, a host of amazing creatures emerge from coral caves and crevices to feed. All the living organisms on the reef depend for their survival on the stony corals which recycle the scarce nutrients from the clear, blue, tropical waters. People, as well as animals, rely on coral reefs for they protect coastlines, attract tourists' money, and some island nations live on coral atolls. Sadly, in spite of being one of the great natural wonders of the world, coral reefs are now under threat. Destruction is caused by reefs being broken up for building materials, damaged by snorkelers and divers touching or treading on them, dynamited by fishermen, ripped up by souvenir collectors, covered by soil eroded by the destruction of rain forests, and polluted by sewage and oil spills.

Green color helps camouflage sea slug among seaweeds

Tentacles of sea anemone covered with stings to put off predators

Large eye for keeping a watch for danger

The clown fish's slimy coat does not trigger the anemone's stings

FRILLY LETTUCE
Sea slugs are related to sea snails but do not have shells. Many sea slugs living on coral reefs feed on corals, but the lettuce slug feeds on algae growing on the reef by sucking the sap from individual cells. Chloroplasts, the green part of plant cells, are then stored in the slug's digestive system where they continue to trap energy from sunlight to make food. Many other reef sea slugs are brightly colored to warn that they are dangerous and recycle the stings that they eat from the coral's tentacles.

Side fin used to steer and change direction

Stripes break up clown fish's outline, perhaps making it more difficult for predators to see the fish on the reef

LIVING IN HARMONY
Clown fish which shelter in anemones live on coral reefs in the Pacific and Indian Oceans. Unlike other fish, clown fish are not stung by their anemone home. The anemone's stings are not triggered because chemicals taken from the anemone are carried in the clown fish's slimy coat. Clown fish seldom venture far from their anemone home for fear of attack by other fish. There are different kinds of clown fish, some living only with certain kinds of anemones.

DATE MUSSEL
Many different clams live on coral reefs. This date mussel makes its home by producing chemicals to wear a hole in the hard coral. Like most clams, the mussel feeds by collecting food particles from water passing through its gills.

Date mussel on a coral reef in the Red Sea

Narrow snout probes for sponges and other animals that grow on rocks

Bright colors help attract a mate

Plain yellow caudal (tail) fin

Adult emperor angelfish's colors and patterns act as signals to other angelfish

Adult

Special glands in skin make slug taste bad to deter predators

GROWING UP
Angelfish are common inhabitants of coral reefs. The young emperor angelfish looks quite different from the adult, possibly because its colors protect it better. Once the adults pair up, they establish a territory on the reef where they can feed. Their colors and patterns help other emperors to recognize them, so they can see their patch of the reef is occupied.

Juvenile

Ring patterns may draw predator away from juvenile's more vulnerable head

Soft body has no shell to protect slug

Flat, slimy foot enables slug to crawl over slippery seaweed

Bright green color shows slug eats algae

NOTORIOUS STARFISH
The crown-of-thorns starfish devours the soft parts of a gorgonian coral. Like many other starfish, it feeds by turning its stomach inside out, making enzymes to digest its prey. Plagues of these starfish attacked Australia's Great Barrier Reef in the 1960s and 1970s, killing large numbers of corals.

Crown-of-thorns starfish eating coral

Lettuce slug breathes through its skin, which looks like the leaf of a plant

Tentacles around mouth used for feeding

Tentacles can be pulled back inside body for protection

Tough skin

One of five rows of tube-feet helps sea cucumber crawl

COLORFUL CUCUMBER
One of the most colorful kinds of sea cucumber lives on or close to reefs in the Indo-Pacific region. Sea cucumbers are echinoderms (pp.18–19), like starfish, sea urchins, and sea lilies. The sea cucumber puts out its sticky tentacles to feed on small particles of food. Once the food has stuck onto the mucus on the tentacle, it is placed inside the mouth and the food removed.

Special fat tentacles for smelling food

Sea meadows

THE MOST ABUNDANT PLANTS IN THE OCEAN are too small to be seen with the naked eye. Often single-celled, these minute, floating plants are called phytoplankton. Like all plants they need sunlight to grow, so are only found in the ocean's upper zone. With the right conditions, phytoplankton multiply quickly—within a few days—as each cell divides into two, and so on. To grow, phytoplankton need nutrients from seawater and lots of sunlight. The most light occurs in the tropics but nutrients, especially nitrogen and phosphorus, are in short supply, restricting phytoplankton's growth. Spectacular phytoplankton blooms are found in cooler waters where nutrients (dead plant and animal waste) are brought up from the bottom during storms, and in both cool and warm waters where there are upwellings of nutrient-rich water. Phytoplankton are eaten by swarms of tiny, drifting animals (zooplankton), which provide a feast for small fish (such as herring), which in turn are eaten by larger fish (such as salmon), which in their turn are eaten by still larger fish or other predators (such as dolphins). Some larger ocean animals (whale sharks and blue whales) feed directly on zooplankton.

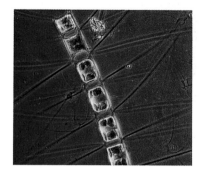

PLANT FOOD
This diatom is one of many phytoplankton that drift in the ocean. Diatoms are the most common kinds of phytoplankton in cooler waters, but dinoflagellates, called single-celled plants, are common in tropical waters. Many diatoms are single cells, but this one consists of a chain of cells.

Glass jar to collect plankton sample

Plankton enters net at wide end

Older stage crab larva showing pincers

IN THE NET
Plankton nets are towed behind a ship or hung from a pier. Studying plankton is important because commercial fish stocks are affected by how much plankton there is for young fish to eat. Changes in plankton can affect the world's climate—phytoplankton play a major role in regulating our climate because they use so much carbon dioxide—one of the gases responsible for global warming.

Very fine mesh net for catching tiny plants and animals drifting in the ocean

Younger stage crab larva

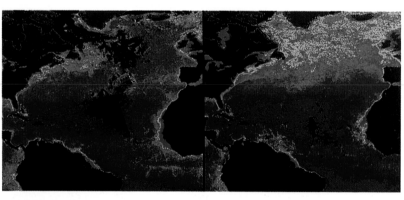

OCEAN IN BLOOM
Images from data collected from a space satellite (*Nimbus 7*) show densities of phytoplankton in the Atlantic Ocean. Red shows where phytoplankton is densest through yellow, green, blue to violet where phytoplankton is least dense. Phytoplankton's spring bloom (right) occurs when days are longer and more nutrients come up from the bottom. A second, smaller bloom of phytoplankton occurs in the fall. When phytoplankton dies, it sinks to the seabed with gelatinous zooplankton remains, making sticky clumps called marine "snow."

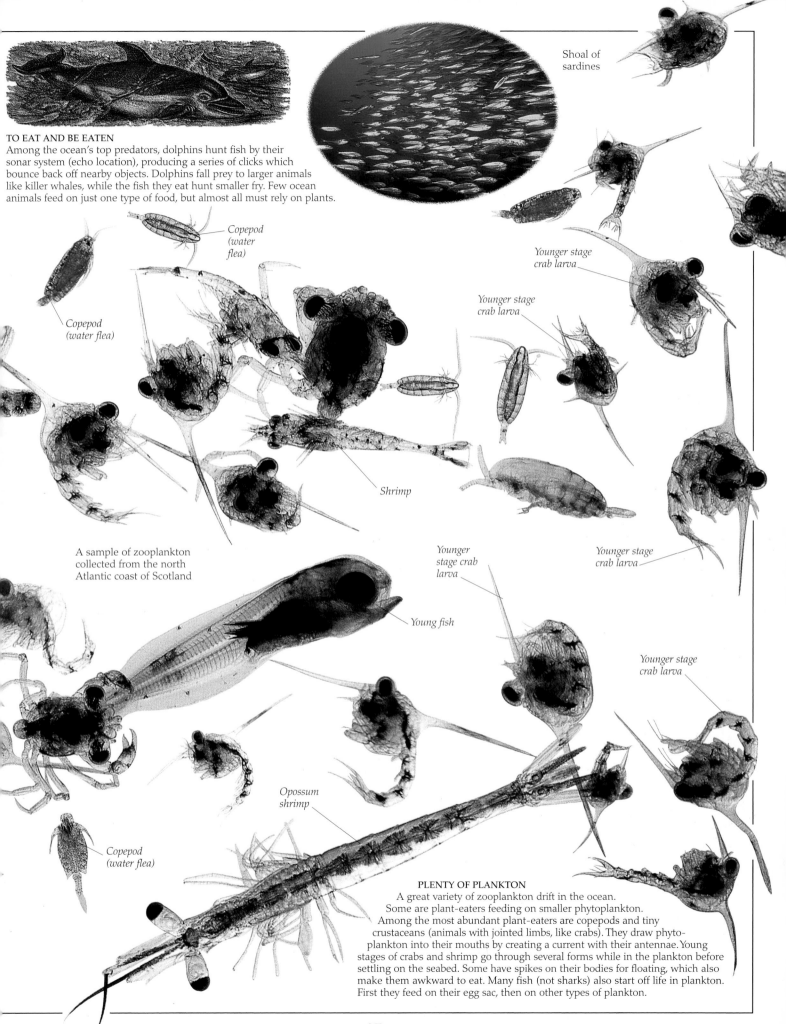

TO EAT AND BE EATEN

Among the ocean's top predators, dolphins hunt fish by their sonar system (echo location), producing a series of clicks which bounce back off nearby objects. Dolphins fall prey to larger animals like killer whales, while the fish they eat hunt smaller fry. Few ocean animals feed on just one type of food, but almost all must rely on plants.

Shoal of sardines

Copepod (water flea)

Copepod (water flea)

Younger stage crab larva

Younger stage crab larva

Shrimp

A sample of zooplankton collected from the north Atlantic coast of Scotland

Younger stage crab larva

Younger stage crab larva

Young fish

Younger stage crab larva

Copepod (water flea)

Opossum shrimp

PLENTY OF PLANKTON

A great variety of zooplankton drift in the ocean. Some are plant-eaters feeding on smaller phytoplankton. Among the most abundant plant-eaters are copepods and tiny crustaceans (animals with jointed limbs, like crabs). They draw phytoplankton into their mouths by creating a current with their antennae. Young stages of crabs and shrimp go through several forms while in the plankton before settling on the seabed. Some have spikes on their bodies for floating, which also make them awkward to eat. Many fish (not sharks) also start off life in plankton. First they feed on their egg sac, then on other types of plankton.

Predators and prey

SOME OCEAN ANIMALS are herbivores (plant-eaters) from certain fish nibbling seaweeds on coral reefs to dugongs chewing seagrasses. There are also many carnivores (meat-eaters) in the ocean. Some, such as blue sharks and barracuda, are swift hunters, while others, such as anglerfish and sea anemones, set traps for their prey waiting with snapping jaws or stinging tentacles respectively. Many animals strain food out of the water from the humble sea fan to giant baleen whales. Seabirds also find their meals in the ocean diving for a beakful of prey. Some ocean animals are omnivores— they eat both plants and animals.

COOPERATIVE FEEDING
Humpback whales herd shoals of fish by letting out bubbles as they swim around them. Opening their mouths wide to gulp in food and water, they retain fish but expel water through sievelike baleen plates in their mouths.

Tiny prey caught in mucus

CAUGHT BY SLIME
Unlike many jellyfish that trap prey with their stinging tentacles, common jellyfish catch small drifting animals (plankton) in sticky slime (mucus) produced by the bell. The four fleshy arms beneath the bell collect up the food-laden slime and tiny hairlike cilia channel it into the mouth.

FANG FACE
The wolf fish has strong, fanglike teeth for crunching through the hard shells of crabs, sea urchins, and mussels. As the front set are worn down each year, or broken, they are replaced by a new set which grow in behind the old teeth. Wolf fish live in cool, deep, northern waters where they lurk in rocky holes.

Dorsal fin runs along entire length of body

Crooked, yellow fanglike teeth

Pectoral fin

Tough, wrinkled skin helps protect wolf fish living near the seabed

Spines to protect urchin

GRAZING AWAY

The European common sea urchin grazes on seaweeds and animals such as sea mats that grow on the surface of seaweeds. The urchin uses the rasping teeth on the underside of its shell that are operated by a complex set of jaws inside, known as Aristotle's lantern. The grazing activities of urchins can control how much seaweed grows in an area, so if too many urchins are collected for food or tourist souvenirs, a rocky reef can become overgrown by seaweed.

Pelican diving

Brown pelican catches fish in beak

Tube-feet used to walk slowly along the seabed

Sea urchin's mouth surrounded by five rasping teeth

FEEDING ON FISHES

Like all pelicans, the brown pelican has a big beak with a large flap of skin or pouch to capture a variety of fish. Once they have spotted their prey, they dive into the water, but are too bulky to dive too far below the surface. Only brown pelicans dive for their prey. When the pelican surfaces, water is drained from the pouch and the fish swallowed.

Tiny teeth of a basking shark

Tiger shark's tooth

TO BITE OR NOT TO BITE

A tiger shark's tooth is like a multipurpose tool with a sharp point for piercing prey and a serrated bladelike edge for slicing. This shark can eat almost anything from hard-shelled turtles to soft-bodied seals and seabirds. The rows of a basking shark's tiny teeth are not used at all, since this shark filters food out of the water with a sieve of gill rakers.

Stinging tentacle

TENTACLE TRAPS

The flowerlike Dahlia anemones are deadly traps for unwary prawns and small fish that stray too close to their stinging tentacles. When the prey brushes past, hundreds of nematocysts (stinging cells) are triggered and fire their stings. These stings ensnare and weaken the prey. The tentacles pass the stricken prey toward the mouth in the anemone's centre—the entrance to the baglike stomach where the prey is digested.

Any undigested pieces of food are ejected through the mouth

Suckerlike disk lets Dahlia anemone attach to any hard surface

Homes and hiding

Staying hidden is one of the best means of defense—
if a predator cannot see you, it cannot eat you! Many sea
animals shelter among seaweeds, in rocky crevices, or under
the sand. Matching the colors and even the texture
of the background also helps sea creatures remain
undetected. The sargassum fish even looks like
bits of seaweed. Hard shells are useful armor, at
least giving protection from weak-jawed predators.
Sea snails and clams make their own shells that
cover the body. Crab and lobsters have outer
shells, like suits of armor, covering the body and
each jointed limb. The hermit crab is unusual because
only the front part of the body and the legs are covered by
a hard shell. Its abdomen is soft, so a hermit crab uses the
empty shell of a sea snail to protect itself.

WHAT A WEED
This fish lives among floating clumps of sargassum
seaweed, where frilly growths on its head, body,
and fins help it avoid being seen by predators,
making a realistic disguise. Many different animals
live in sargassum seaweed, which drifts in large
quantities in the Sargasso Sea of the North Atlantic.

BLENDING IN
Cuttlefish have different colored
pigments and rapidly change color
to escape predators. Their eyes
perceive their surroundings
and nerve signals are sent
by the brain to tiny bags
of pigment in the skin.
When these pigment
bags contract, the
cuttlefish's color
becomes lighter.

*Cuttlefish
becomes
darker when
pigment bags
expand*

*Hermit crab
leaving old
whelk shell*

Anemone

*Investigating its new
home by checking size
with its claws*

Hermit crab can be
persuaded to move
into a perspex shell so
its movements can
be viewed

*When out of its shell,
crab is vulnerable to
predators*

ALL CHANGE
Like all crustaceans, a hermit crab grows by shedding its hard,
outer skeleton and does this within the safety of its snail shell
home. As it grows larger, it needs to find a larger snail shell to
move into. Before leaving its old shell, it will test the size of a
new home. If it is not large enough or is cracked, the hermit
crab looks for another shell. When the hermit crab has found
one which is just right, it carefully pulls its body out of its old
shell, tucking it quickly into the new shell. As the hermit crab
grows larger it moves into large whelk shells and lives
in shallow water submerged on the seabed.

*Leg with
pointed claws
to get a grip on
seabed when
walking*

Antenna

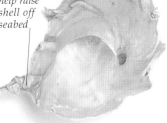

Points on bottom edge help raise shell off seabed

SHELLS ON SHELLS
Carrier shells are sea snails that attach empty shells and bits of hard debris, including corals, pebbles, and even broken glass, to their own shells. This disguise is to hide them from predators such as fish. The extra projections may make it more difficult for predators to crack open the shells to reach the soft meat inside.

Tip of abdomen (the tail-end of the body) has an appendage to grip inner whorl of shell

Abdomen brought forward to shell opening to deposit droppings, so crab does not foul its shell

Pincer also used to pick up food

ANOTHER HOME
Some kinds of hermit crab do not move home, but make extensions to their shells by placing a cloak anemone near the shell's entrance. Others just place anemones on top of their shells using their stings for protection, while the anemone picks up scraps of food from the crab. Worms sometimes make their homes inside the shell of the hermit crab, even stealing food from them.

Soft body of crab winds around shell's spirals

Large pincer, or cheliped, used to block entrance to shell, so providing extra security

HOME, SWEET HOME
The European hermit crab first makes its home in smaller shells, such as those of the topshell or periwinkle, which the crab finds on the shore. When it grows larger, the hermit crab usually lives in whelk shells. Hermit crabs carry their homes around with them and females of the species rear the eggs inside their shells.

Attack and defense

MANY SEA CREATURES HAVE WEAPONS to defend themselves from predators or to attack prey. Some produce venom (poison) for defense and often advertise their danger with distinctive markings. Lionfish's stripes may alert enemies to their venomous spines, but being easy to see, they hunt at dusk and during the night when they can still surprise their prey out in the open. Stonefish are armed with venomous spines, too, blending perfectly with their background when waiting on a reef for prey to swim by. Octopuses change color to that of their background. If attacked, the blue-ringed octopus produces blue spots to warn that its bite is poisonous. Disappearing in a cloud of ink is another useful trick used by octopuses, squid, and cuttlefish. Most clams can withdraw their delicate soft parts into their shells, but the gaping file shell's tentacles are a deterrent producing an irritating sticky fluid. But no defense method is foolproof. Even the most venomous jellyfish can be eaten by carnivorous turtles that are immune to their stings.

DEADLY STONEFISH
The stonefish is one of the most deadly creatures in the ocean. A stonefish's venom, which is injected through the sharp spines on its back, causes such intense pain that a person stepping on one may go into shock and die.

Ink cloud forming around cuttlefish

Long, dorsal spine with venom glands in grooves

INK SCREEN
Cephalopods, which include cuttlefish, squid, and octopuses, produce a cloud of ink when threatened, to confuse an enemy and allow time for escape. The ink, produced in a gland linked to the gut, is ejected in a blast of water from a tubelike funnel near its head.

Horny projection above eye

Maerl (a chalky, red seaweed) grows in a thick mass along the stony seabed

Three venomous anal spines

KEEP CLEAR
The striped body of lionfish warns predators that they are dangerous. A predator trying to bite a lionfish may be impaled by one or more of its poisonous spines. If it survives, the predator will remember the danger and leave the lionfish alone in future. Lionfish can swim openly looking for smaller prey with little risk of attack. They live in tropical waters from the Indian to the Pacific Oceans. In spite of being poisonous, they are popular aquarium fish because of their beauty.

Stripes warn predators that lionfish is dangerous

BLUE FOR DANGER
If this octopus becomes irritated, or when it is feeding, blue-ringed spots appear on its skin, warning of its poisonous bite. This octopus is only about the size of a person's hand, but its bite can be fatal. One kind of blue-ringed octopus lives in cool shallow waters around parts of Australia. Others are found in tropical waters.

*Two venomous spines
on tail can pierce the
swimmer's skin and
inject its venom*

Painting of
sea monsters,
c. 1880s

*Sting ray's sting is
sharp and serrated
so it can easily
pierce the skin*

*Pectoral
fin used for
swimming*

STING IN THE TAIL
This blue-spotted ray lives in
the warm waters of both the
Indian and Pacific Oceans as well as
the Red Sea, where it is often found
lurking on the sandy seabed. If stepped on,
shooting pains occur in the foot for over an hour,
but, after several hours, the pain gradually wears off.

SOMETHING SCARY
Early sailors knew that some creatures living in
the sea were dangerous and could kill people.
Tales about these sea monsters, though common,
often became greatly exaggerated. Monster
stories were also invented to account for ships that
foundered due to dangerous sea conditions.

VICIOUS JELLYFISH
Jellyfish are well-known for their
nasty stings, but the nastiest are
those of the box jellyfish, which
swim near the coasts of northern
Australia and southeast Asia. Its
stings produce horrible welts on
anyone who comes in contact
with their tentacles. A badly
stung person can die in
four minutes.

*When shell is closed, there
is still a gap between the
shell's two halves*

*Tentacles
always
on show*

SHAGGY SHELLS
These gaping file shells cannot withdraw
their masses of orange tentacles inside the
two halves of their shell for protection, so
the tentacles produce a sour-tasting, sticky
substance to deter predators. If tentacles
are nibbled off, they can regrow. Gaping
file shells build homes in seaweed,
by putting out byssus threads for
anchorage. They can also make
"nests" among horse mussels and
oarweeds. If dislodged from
their homes, they can move by
expelling water from their
shell and using their
tentacles like oars.

*Shell is
up to 1 in
(2.5) long*

The jet set

ONE WAY TO GET AROUND QUICKLY in water is by jet propulsion. Some mollusks, such as clams, squid, and octopuses, do this by squirting water from the body cavity. Jet propulsion can be used both for swimming and to help mollusks escape from predators. Squid are best at jet propulsion—their bodies are permanently streamlined to reduce drag (resistance to water). Some kinds of scallops also use jet propulsion and are among the few clams that can swim. Most clams (bivalves with shells in two halves) can only bury themselves in the sand, or are anchored to the seabed. The common octopus lives on the rocky seabed in the coastal waters of the Atlantic Ocean, and the Mediterranean and Caribbean seas. If attacked, it can jet off.

TENTACLE TALES
A Norwegian story tells of the Kraken, a giant sea monster that wrapped its arms around ships before sinking them. The legend may be based on the mysterious giant squid which live in deep waters. Dead individuals sometimes are seen washed up on the shore. In 2004 the first living one was caught in the depths by one of its tentacles and photographed as it escaped.

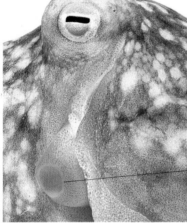

Funnel

JET PROPULSION
The engines powering jet planes produce jets of air to fly in much the same way that octopuses, squid, and cuttlefish produce jets of water to propel themselves through the sea.

Long arms to grasp prey

FLEXIBLE FUNNEL
Sticking out from the edge of the octopus's baglike body is its funnel. The funnel can be bent so the jet of water can be aimed backward or forward, to control the direction in which the octopus heads off.

1 ON THE BOTTOM
The common octopus hides during the day in its rocky lair, coming out at night to look for such food as crustaceans. The octopus slowly approaches its prey, then pounces, wrapping it between the webbing at the base of its arms.

Powerful suckers grip the rock, so octopus can pull itself along

Sucker is sensitive to touch and taste

34

Tentacles trail out behind body, when octopus takes off

2 OFF THE BOTTOM

If possible an octopus keeps one arm fixed to a surface, so it can pull itself down to the seabed to hide. To move slowly off the bottom, the octopus squirts water gently out of its funnel, but to travel at speed it moves with its arms trailing behind.

3 FAST RETREAT

If threatened, the octopus jets off, making its baglike body streamlined to reduce drag in the water. To keep swimming, the octopus's body pulsates. It takes water into the body cavity, forcing it out through the funnel. Octopuses may also eject a cloud of ink to confuse any attackers.

Eye is similar to human eye and is used to spot prey

Eyes around edge of shell can detect shadow of a fish passing overhead

Scallop moving

Hinge

Water jets near hinge propel scallop forward when swimming

Two rows of suckers underneath each arm

Arm can reach out to take hold of prey or investigate a potential meal

Each octopus has eight arms

Scallop shell is made of two halves called valves

When swimming, a scallop looks like a pair of false teeth taking "bites" out of the water

Scallop partly open

Sensory tentacles

Edge of mantle (skin) covers the scallop's body and makes its shell

IN THE SWIM

Scallops launch themselves off the bottom by squeezing water out of their shells. When swimming from place to place, streams of water are aimed out of the back of the shell on either side of the hinge. Shoals of scallops may take off and swim together. If a predator approaches, such as a starfish, the scallop shoots a jet of water out of the front of the shell and zips off with the hinge in front.

Scallops on the seabed

Moving along

AT SCHOOL
Fish often swim together in a shoal or school (like these blue-striped snappers), where a single fish has less chance of being attacked by a predator than when swimming on its own. The moving mass of individuals may confuse a predator and also there are more pairs of eyes on the lookout for an attacker.

EVERY SWIMMER KNOWS that it is harder to move an arm or a leg through seawater than through air. This is because seawater is much denser than air. To be a fast swimmer like a dolphin, tuna, or sailfish, it helps to have a shape that is streamlined like a torpedo to reduce drag (resistance to water). A smooth skin and few projections from the body allow an animal to move through the water more easily. The density of seawater does have an advantage, in that it helps to support the weight of an animal's body. The heaviest animal that ever lived on Earth is the blue whale, which weighs up to 165 tons (150 metric tons). Some heavy-shelled creatures, like the chambered nautilus, have gas-filled floats to stop them from sinking. Some ocean animals, such as dolphins and flying fish, get up enough speed under water to leap briefly into the air, but not all ocean animals are good swimmers. Many can only swim slowly, some drift along in the currents, crawl along the bottom, burrow in the sand, or stay put, anchored to the seabed.

IN THE SWING
During the day, many electric rays prefer to stay hidden on the sandy bottom, as well as relying on their electric organs for defense, but they do swim if disturbed and at night when searching for prey. There are about 20 members of the electric ray family, mostly living in warm waters. Most other rays have spindly tails (unlike the electric ray's broad tail), so move through water using their pectoral fins. Waves pass from the front to the back of the pectoral fins which, in larger rays such as mantas, become so exaggerated that the fins actually beat up and down.

Electric ray's smooth skin can be either blackish or red-brown in color

Spiracle (a one-way valve) takes in water which is pumped out through gill slits underneath

Some electric rays can grow to 6 ft (1.8 m) and weigh as much as 110 lb (50 kg)

Pelvic fin

Swimming sequence of an electric ray

DIVING DEEP
True seals use front flippers to steer through the water. They move by beating their back flippers and tail from side to side. Their nostrils are closed to prevent water entering the airways. Harbor seals (right) can dive to 300 ft (90 m), but the champion seal diver is the elephant seal, diving to over 5,000 ft (1,500 m). Seals do not get the bends because their lungs collapse early in the dive and, unlike humans, they do not breathe compressed air. When underwater, seals use oxygen stored in the blood.

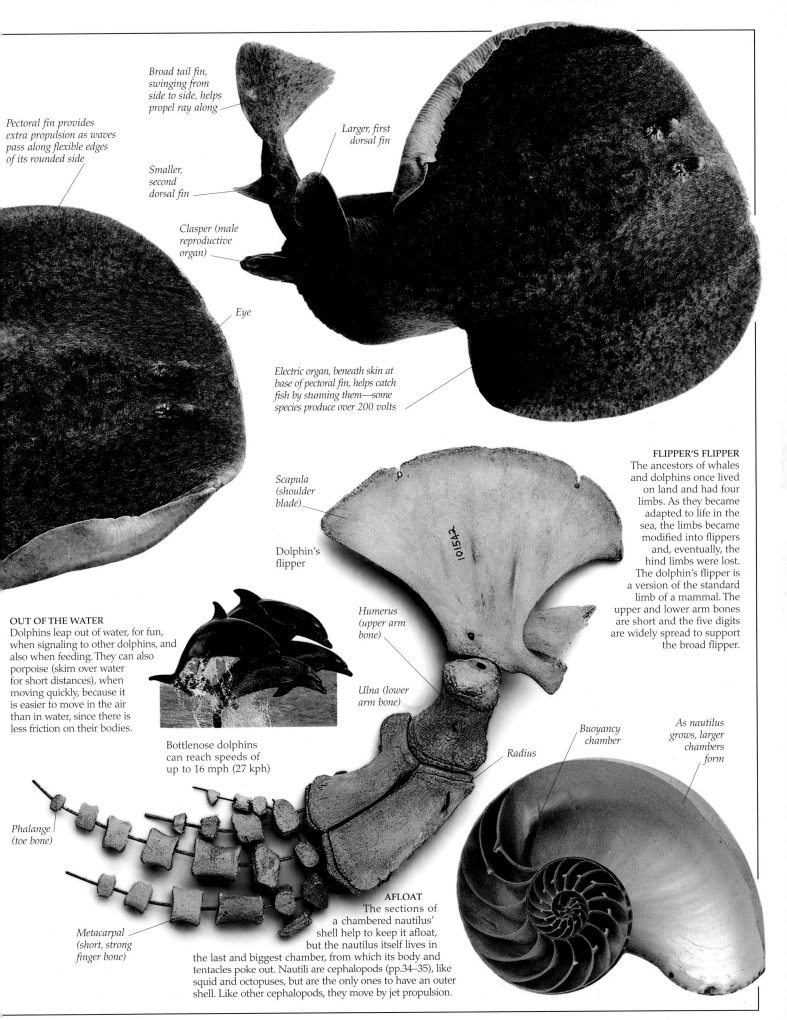

Broad tail fin, swinging from side to side, helps propel ray along

Pectoral fin provides extra propulsion as waves pass along flexible edges of its rounded side

Smaller, second dorsal fin

Larger, first dorsal fin

Clasper (male reproductive organ)

Eye

Electric organ, beneath skin at base of pectoral fin, helps catch fish by stunning them—some species produce over 200 volts

Scapula (shoulder blade)

Dolphin's flipper

FLIPPER'S FLIPPER
The ancestors of whales and dolphins once lived on land and had four limbs. As they became adapted to life in the sea, the limbs became modified into flippers and, eventually, the hind limbs were lost. The dolphin's flipper is a version of the standard limb of a mammal. The upper and lower arm bones are short and the five digits are widely spread to support the broad flipper.

Humerus (upper arm bone)

Ulna (lower arm bone)

OUT OF THE WATER
Dolphins leap out of water, for fun, when signaling to other dolphins, and also when feeding. They can also porpoise (skim over water for short distances), when moving quickly, because it is easier to move in the air than in water, since there is less friction on their bodies.

Bottlenose dolphins can reach speeds of up to 16 mph (27 kph)

Buoyancy chamber

As nautilus grows, larger chambers form

Radius

Phalange (toe bone)

Metacarpal (short, strong finger bone)

AFLOAT
The sections of a chambered nautilus' shell help to keep it afloat, but the nautilus itself lives in the last and biggest chamber, from which its body and tentacles poke out. Nautili are cephalopods (pp.34–35), like squid and octopuses, but are the only ones to have an outer shell. Like other cephalopods, they move by jet propulsion.

Ocean travelers

To make the most of the vast expanses of water, some sea animals travel great distances, crisscrossing the oceans to find the best places to feed and breed. Whales, like the humpback, are known for feeding in the cold, food-rich waters of the far north or south, traveling to the warm waters of the tropics to breed and give birth. Many long-distance voyagers, such as turtles, seals, and seabirds, feed out at sea, but come ashore to breed. Freshwater eels are unusual because they go to the ocean to breed, then their young travel back to rivers where they grow to maturity. Salmon do the reverse, growing in the ocean and returning to rivers to breed. Ocean travelers often make use of currents to speed them on their way. Even animals that cannot swim can travel far and wide by hitching a ride on another animal or by drifting along on a piece of wood.

Back pair of flippers used as rudders to steer turtle along

Stalked barnacles on driftwood

BARNACLES ADRIFT
Barnacles grow on surfaces, such as rocks, pieces of wood, hulls of ships, and some kinds even grow on turtles and whales. These goose barnacles can drift long distance on pieces of wood. Barnacles are crustaceans (like crabs and lobsters) and have jointed limbs. To protect their bodies and limbs, barnacles have a set of shelllike plates.

Broad surface of front flipper for ease of swimming.

Larger eyes form when adult eel migrates to sea

Leaflike larva (young), called Leptocephalus

Trailing tentacles armed with vicious stings

Skin turns silver before eel migrates back to Sargasso Sea

Young eels, known as elvers or glass eels

MYSTERIOUS JOURNEY
For centuries, no one knew where European eels went to breed, only that young eels returned in large numbers to the rivers. In the late 1800s, scientists found leaflike larvae in the sea which developed into elvers. Later they found that the smallest larvae came from the Sargasso Sea in the western Atlantic where adult eels may breed at depth. The larvae then drift with currents back to the European coast where they turn into elvers.

PORTUGUESE MAN-OF-WAR
Not a true jellyfish but a siphonophore (a relative of sea firs), the man-of-war has a gas-filled float which keeps it at the surface where it is blown by the wind and drifts with the currents. Usually found in warm waters, it can be carried to cooler waters and washed ashore after storms.

Swimming sequence
of a green turtle

*Turtle shell is
streamlined for
gliding through
water*

UNDERWATER FLIER

Green turtles live in warm waters in the Atlantic, Pacific, and
Indian Oceans. Like all turtles, they come ashore to lay their
eggs. First the females mate in shallow water with the waiting
males. Later, under cover of darkness, the females crawl up
the beach to lay their eggs in the sand before heading back
to the water. They may return several times in one
breeding season to lay further batches of eggs.
Some green turtles are known to travel
several hundred miles or more to reach
their breeding beaches where they
hatched themselves. Green
turtles feed on sea grasses
and seaweeds.

*Front pair of
flippers help
turtle to "fly"
through water*

*Turtles are
air breathers,
so must come
to surface
to breathe
through their
nostrils*

Green turtle
(*Chelonia mydas*)
is on the
endangered
species list

TURTLE TRIP

In the Japanese legend, Urashima Taro rides into the
kingdom of the sea on a turtle. After spending some time in
the depths, he begs the sea goddess to let him go home. She
allows this, but gives him a box which he must never open.
On his return he finds his home has changed and no one
knows him. Hoping for some comfort, he opens the box but
the spell is broken. He becomes a very old man because
he has spent not three years—but 300—in the sea.

The twilight zone

BETWEEN THE BRIGHT SUNLIT WATERS of the upper ocean and the pitch black depths is the half light of the twilight zone, which ranges from 650 to 3,300 ft (200 to 1,000 m) below the surface. Fish living in the twilight zone often have rows of light organs on their undersides to help camouflage them against the little light filtering down from above. These glowing lights can be produced by chemical reactions or by colonies of bacteria living in the light organs. Many animals, including some lantern fish and a variety of squid, spend only their days in the twilight zone. At night they journey upward to feed in the food-rich surface water. By doing this, they are less at risk from daytime hunters such as seabirds. Others, such as the lancet fish, spend most of their lives in the twilight zone eating any available food. The skinny lancet fish has a stretchy stomach, so takes a large meal if it finds one.

HUNTER OF THE DEPTHS
Viper fish have an impressive set of daggerlike teeth to grab their fish prey, which they attract with a lure dangling from the front of the dorsal fin. The extralong teeth in the bottom jaw are too large to fit inside the mouth when the jaws are closed. When swallowing prey, such as a hatchet fish (above left), the hinged jaws open very wide.

Fin ray

Saillike dorsal fin can be raised and lowered

Jumbo squid can reach 12 ft (3.6 m) to the tips of their tentacles

A GIANT OF A SQUID
Any squid over 20 in (0.5 m) long is big, but the Atlantic giant squid can weigh one ton. Suckers line the arms and tentacles to cling onto prey. Sperm whales often bear sucker-shaped scars where they have grappled with squid (p.34).

Dorsal fin can be used for herding fish prey

MERMAN
Many strange creatures lurk in the ocean depths, but no one is likely to find one looking like this.

Large gill flap

Model of a lancet fish

Pointed teeth for grabbing fish

Pectoral fin

LONG AND SKLNNY
The lancet fish only weighs up to 10 lb (4.5 kg), because it has a narrow body, lightweight bones, and not much muscle. A predator, it catches squid and other fish, such as hatchet fish, living at the same depths.

Pelvic fin

Model of a hatchet
fish, *Sternoptyx*

*Sharply angled
dorsal fin*

*Silvery body helps
camouflage fish in
right light*

*Large eye
helps spot
prey in the
dark*

GLASS JELLIES
Glass jellyfish live in
all the world's oceans.
They are found in the
sunlit upper zone as
well as at depths of
2,300 ft (700 m). They
have a deep bell with
a long mouth hanging
down, which twists
round to catch tiny
prey. Glass jellyfish
can put on displays
of beautiful rainbow
colors.

*Luminous patches
in the mouth can
attract prey right
inside the jaw*

*Light organs
also found under
tail*

DEEP-SEA HATCHET
Hatchet fish have bladelike, silvery
bodies. The light organs along their belly
and tail, when viewed from below, help
them blend in with the brighter surface
water above. These must be the right degree
of brightness so as not to outshine the light
from above, which would make them easier
to see. Hatchet fish live in the Atlantic, Pacific,
and Indian Oceans.

*Light organs
located on belly*

*Upward-pointing
eye helps locate
prey*

*Large, first
dorsal fin*

*Symmetrical
tail fin*

Model of a
hatchet fish,
Opisthoproctus

LOOKING UP
There is more than one type of hatchet fish. This bizarre-
looking hatchet fish has large, tubular eyes pointing upward
so it can see its prey, such as deep-water siphonophores
(jellyfishlike relatives of sea firs). The welldeveloped eyes
can detect the faintest glimmer of their prey's light. This
fish is found in oceans around the world below regions
with warm surface waters.

*Tube along
belly produces
light to avoid
being spotted
from below by
predators*

*Anus
contains a
colony of
luminescent
bacteria that
generate light*

*Asymmetrical
caudal (tail) fin*

*Extremely tiny
second dorsal
fin is fleshy*

*Lancet fish swims
below the warm surface
waters of the Atlantic,
Pacific, and Caribbean*

*Colors (instead of light
organs) help fish blend into
light ocean above and dark
ocean below*

*Lancet fish can
grow to 6 ft 6 in
(2 m) long*

The darkest depths

THERE IS NO LIGHT in the oceans below 3,300 ft (1,000 m), just inky blackness. Many fish in the dark zone are black too, making them almost invisible. Light organs are used as signals to find a mate or to lure prey. Food is scarce in the cold, dark depths. Ultimately, all the animals have to rely on is what little rains down from above. Deep-sea fish make the most of little food by having huge mouths and stretchy stomachs, giving fish a strange appearance. Often they are small or weigh little due to lightweight bones and muscles. Being lightweight helps fish in the dark zone maintain neutral buoyancy (keeping at one level without having to swim), even though most have no gas-filled swim bladders.

Lateral line organs sense vibrations in water made by moving prey

UMBRELLA MOUTH GULPER
With its large mouth opened wide, the gulper eel is always ready to swallow any food, such as shrimp and small fish, it may come across. The gulper probably catches food by swimming along slowly with its mouth open. Adult gulper eels live in the lower part of the twilight zone and in the dark zone. The young stages resemble the leaflike larvae of European eels (pp.38–39) and are found in the sunlit zone from 330–660 ft (100–200 m). As they grow, the young gulper eels descend into deeper water.

Adults grow to about 30 in (75 cm) from heads to tips of their long tails

Tiny eye on end of nose

Gulper eel lives in the dark depths below temperate and tropical surface waters

Long lower jaw

FISHING LINE
The whipnose has a long, whiplike lure for attracting passing prey. Prey is drawn toward the lure, thinking it may be a source of food, then gets snapped up by the whipnose.

Whipnose grows to 5 in (13 cm) in length

MONSTER MOVIES
Films about scary monsters are always popular, especially those from the pitch black ocean depths. Curiously, so little of the deep ocean has been explored that there could be strange animals yet to be discovered. But most deep sea animals are small, because there is so little food at these depths.

Model of a whipnose, which lives in the Atlantic and Pacific Oceans

BINOCULAR EYES
Gigantura's extraordinary tubular eyes are probably used to pinpoint the glowing light organs of its prey. Even though *Gigantura* has a narrow body, its skin can stretch so that it can swallow fish larger than itself.

Lower lobe of tail fin longer than upper lobe

GOING FISHING

Anglerfish are not just found in the ocean depths. This one, from shallow waters, uses a wormlike lure on the end of its dorsal fin ray as a lure. A fish swimming by, tempted to bite the worm, will end inside the angler's stomach.

Model of an anglerfish
(*Melanocetus*)
before a meal

Lure contains luminous bacteria used to attract prey and males

Model of an anglerfish after a meal

Female of anglerfish can grow to 3 in (8 cm) long

Small eye typical of fish of the dark zone

Teeth bend backward allowing passage of large prey into mouth

Caudal fin

DEEP SEA ANGLER

Melanocetus has been found with a lantern fish twice its own size in its stomach. The prey is guided to its gaping jaws by a glow-in-the-dark lure on the end of a long fin ray. Large teeth, curving backward, make sure that the angler does not let go of its prey once it is within its jaws. The prey is not chewed up, but swallowed whole. Male deep sea anglers are up to 20 times smaller than the females and either feed on much smaller prey, such as shrimp, or do not feed at all. Once a dwarf male finds a female he hangs on by his jaws. In some anglers, the male's whole body fuses with hers so he receives food via her bloodstream.

Big, stretchy stomach allows deep sea anglerfish to take huge meals

Extraordinary eyes look like binoculars

Model of *Gigantura*

TOUGH JELLY

Found in all the world's oceans, *Atolla* jellyfish are as tough as fruit gums. The reddish-brown color is typical of deep sea jellyfish. Like most jellyfish, they have stinging tentacles to catch prey. If disturbed, *Atolla* glows in the dark, sending out a bluish light for several seconds.

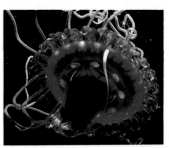

On the bottom

THE BOTTOM OF THE DEEP OCEAN is not an easy place to live. There is little food and it is dark and cold. Much of the seabed is covered with soft clays or mudlike oozes made of skeletons of tiny sea animals and plants. The ooze on the vast open plains of the abyss can reach several hundred yards thick. Animals walking along the bottom have long legs to keep from stirring it up. Some grow anchored to the seabed and have long stems to keep their feeding structures clear of the ooze. Food particles can be filtered out of the water, for example, by the feathery arms in sea lilies or through the many pores in sponges. Some animals, such as sea cucumbers, feed on the seabed and manage to extract enough goodness from food particles within the ooze. Food particles are the remains of dead animals (and their droppings) and plants that have sunk down from above. Occasionally, a larger carcass reaches the bottom uneaten, providing a real bonanza for the mobile bottom-dwellers that home in on it from all around. Because food is scarce and temperatures so low, most animals living in the deep ocean take a long time to grow.

Underwater cables were laid across the Atlantic Ocean to relay telegraphic messages, c. 1870

Dried remains of sea anemones

GLASSY STRANDS
This sponge grows anchored to the soft seabed by its stem of glass strands and sea anemones often grow on their stems. When a glass-rope sponge dies, the cup-shaped part disappears and all that is left is the stem stuck in the seabed.

NOT A TRUE SPIDER
Looking like land spiders, sea spiders belong to a group called pycnogonids. Some deep-sea spiders have a leg span of 2 ft (60 cm) across, and can stride along without stirring up clouds of particles. They can also swim, by launching off the seabed, bringing their legs upward, then sinking down again.

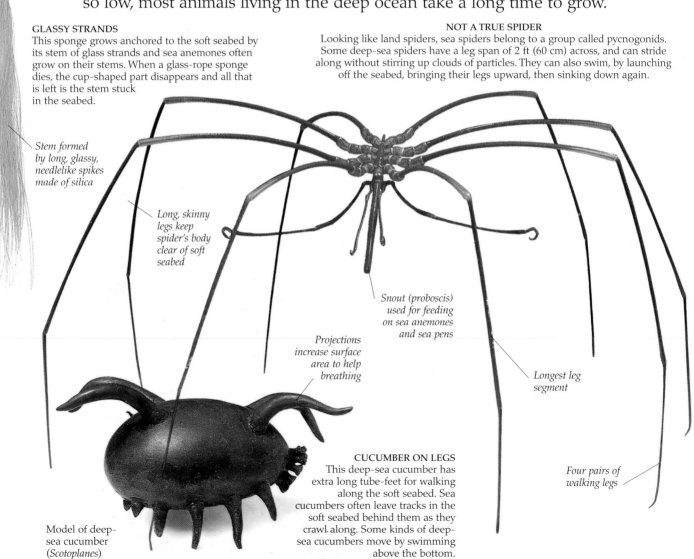

Stem formed by long, glassy, needlelike spikes made of silica

Long, skinny legs keep spider's body clear of soft seabed

Snout (proboscis) used for feeding on sea anemones and sea pens

Projections increase surface area to help breathing

Longest leg segment

CUCUMBER ON LEGS
This deep-sea cucumber has extra long tube-feet for walking along the soft seabed. Sea cucumbers often leave tracks in the soft seabed behind them as they crawl along. Some kinds of deep-sea cucumbers move by swimming above the bottom.

Four pairs of walking legs

Model of deep-sea cucumber (*Scotoplanes*)

Specimens, brought up from the deep, are dried to preserve them

Brittle star's arms wound around sea pen for support

LILY OF THE DEEP
Sea lilies use their feathery arms to gather food particles from the water. Many kinds of sea lilies live on the floor of the deep sea in the trenches—from 300 to over 26,500 ft (100 to over 8,000 m) deep. Some have roots and stems anchored to the seabed, while those with whorls of spikes (cirri) around their stems can move by using their arms, dragging their stems behind them. The spikes along the stem act as props and those at the base of the stem can grip the seabed.

Engraving of deep-sea lily

Dried specimens of deep-sea brittle stars (*Asteronyx loveni*)

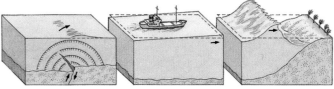

STARTING ON THE BOTTOM
Tsunamis are often called tidal waves, but they are not caused by tides. They begin because of earthquakes or eruptions on the seabed, sending out shock waves through the water. Traveling across the open sea at great speed, the waves are usually around 2 ft (0.5 m) high. When they near the coast, they bunch up to make towering walls of water that can devastate anything on land.

Long arms can grasp food drifting by in the water

Stem of sea pen grows up from the seabed

FLOWER BASKETS
The glassy skeletons of Venus flower basket sponges have long been admired for their beauty. The Japanese viewed them as symbols of wedded bliss, because pairs of shrimps were often found inside them. The living sponge is not as attractive because it is covered with soft tissues. Most glass sponges live in deep waters, but some live in shallower waters in cold, polar regions.

Opening of sponge covered with sieve plate

Glassy skeleton

ALL IN THE ARMS
These deep-sea brittle stars are usually found wound around sea pens on the ocean floor. They use their long, snakelike arms to cling onto the sea pen and to feed on small creatures and other food particles drifting by. Climbing off the seabed gives the brittle stars a better chance to collect food. Brittle stars and sea pens are common bottom-dwellers from shallow water to the deep sea in oceans around the world. These deep-sea brittle stars live at depths of 300–6,000 ft (100–1,800 m).

Victorian display of a dried Venus flower basket (*Euplectella aspergillium*)

Vents and smokers

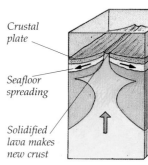

Crustal plate

Seafloor spreading

Solidified lava makes new crust

IN PARTS OF THE OCEAN FLOOR, there are cracks from which very hot, mineral-rich water gushes. These vents, or hot springs, exist at the spreading centers where gigantic plates that make up the Earth's crust are moving apart. Cold seawater sinks deep into cracks in the crust where the water is heated, collecting dissolved minerals. At temperatures of up to 750°F (400°C), hot water spews out and some of the minerals form chimneys (black smokers). Hot water produced by vents helps bacteria to grow, which create food from the hydrogen sulfide in the water. Extraordinary animals crowd around the cracks and rely on these microbes for food. In the late 1970s, scientists using submersibles discovered the first vent communities in the Pacific. Since then, vents have been discovered in other spreading centers in the Pacific and the Mid-Atlantic Ridge.

GROWING OCEAN
New areas of ocean floor are continually being created at spreading centers between two crustal plates. When hot, molten rock (lava) emerges from within the crust, the lava cools and solidifies adding material to the edge of each adjoining plate. Old areas of ocean floor are destroyed where one plate slides under another. Lava from volcanic eruptions at spreading centers can kill off communities of vent animals.

Animals cook if too close to hot water in a vent

Plumes of hot water are rich in sulfides, which are poisonous to most animals

Fish predators nibble tops off tube worms

Dense numbers of animals crowd around a vent

BLACK SMOKER
Animal life abounds in an active vent site, such as this one in the Mid-Atlantic Ridge. If the vent stops producing hot, sulfur-rich water, the community is doomed. Animals from dying vents must colonize a new site, which may be several hundred miles away across the cold, almost barren seafloor.

Giant clams in the eastern Pacific can grow to 12 in (30 cm) long

Some animals graze on mats of bacteria covering rocks near a vent

Model of hydro-thermal vents found in the eastern Pacific

Deep-sea fish photographed from Alvin near a vent on the Mid-Atlantic Ridge

Alvin by the support ship, Atlantis II

Chimney made from mineral deposits

Black smoker chimney can reach over 30 ft (10 m) high

CHAMPION SUBMERSIBLE
The US submersible, *Alvin,* was the first to take scientists down to observe marine life near the Galapagos vents in the east Pacific in the 1970s. Since then, *Alvin* has completed many dives to vents around the world to depths of 12,500 ft (3,800 m). Other submersibles that have dived on vent sites include the French *Nautile* (pp.54–55) and the Russian *Mir I* and *II.*

VENT COMMUNITIES
This model shows the vent communities in the eastern Pacific, where giant clams and tube worms are the most distinctive animals. Vents in other parts of the world have different groups of animals, such as the hairy snails from the Mariana Trench and eyeless shrimps from vents along the Mid-Atlantic Ridge.

Tube worm can grow to 10 ft (3 m) long

Giant tube worm has bacteria inside its body, which provides the worm with food

Diverse divers

PEOPLE HAVE ALWAYS WANTED to explore the sea, to look for sunken treasure, to salvage wrecks, to bring up marine products like pearls and sponges, or to examine the beautiful underwater world. Recently, underwater oil exploration and drilling have also required divers' skills. The first diving equipment were simple bells, containing air and open at the bottom so the diver could work on the seabed. Later, diving suits with hard helmets were invented to enable divers to go deeper and stay down longer, with air pumped continually down a line from the surface. In the 1940s, the modern aqualung or SCUBA (Self-Contained Underwater Breathing Apparatus) was invented. Divers could carry their own supply of compressed air in tanks on their backs.

Umbilical supplies air and electricity for light

Weight belt

UNDERWATER WORKER
This diver, wearing a wetsuit for warmth, gets air into the helmet via a line linked to the surface. A harness goes around the diver's middle to carry tools. Flexible boots help the diver clamber around beneath an oil rig.

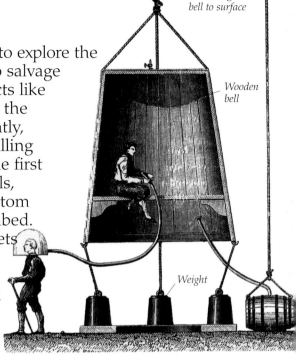

Rope connecting bell to surface

Wooden bell

Weight

EARLY DIVING BELL
In 1690, Edmund Halley invented a diving bell, allowing a diver to be resupplied with barrels of air lowered from the surface. The bell, open at the bottom, was anchored to the seabed by heavy weights. A leather tube connected the lead-lined air barrel to the wooden bell. Several divers at a time could work from the bell which was used at depths of 60 ft (18 m).

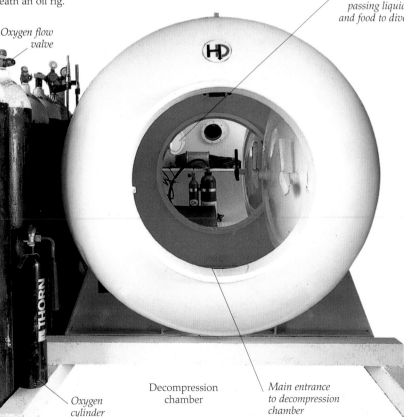

"Medical lock" for passing liquids and food to diver

Oxygen flow valve

Oxygen cylinder

Decompression chamber

Main entrance to decompression chamber

Joint pains indicate decompression sickness

LIFE SAVER
When diving, the pressure on the body increases due to the weight of water above the diver. The air is supplied under the same pressure so the diver can breathe. With this increased pressure, the nitrogen in the air supply (air contains 80 percent nitrogen) passes into the blood. If a diver comes up too quickly after a long or deep dive, the sudden release of pressure can cause nitrogen to form bubbles in the blood and tissues. This painful, sometimes fatal condition is called decompression sickness (the bends). The ailing diver is treated in a decompression chamber. The pressure is raised to the level required to move bubbles out through the lungs, and then is slowly reduced to normal pressure at the surface.

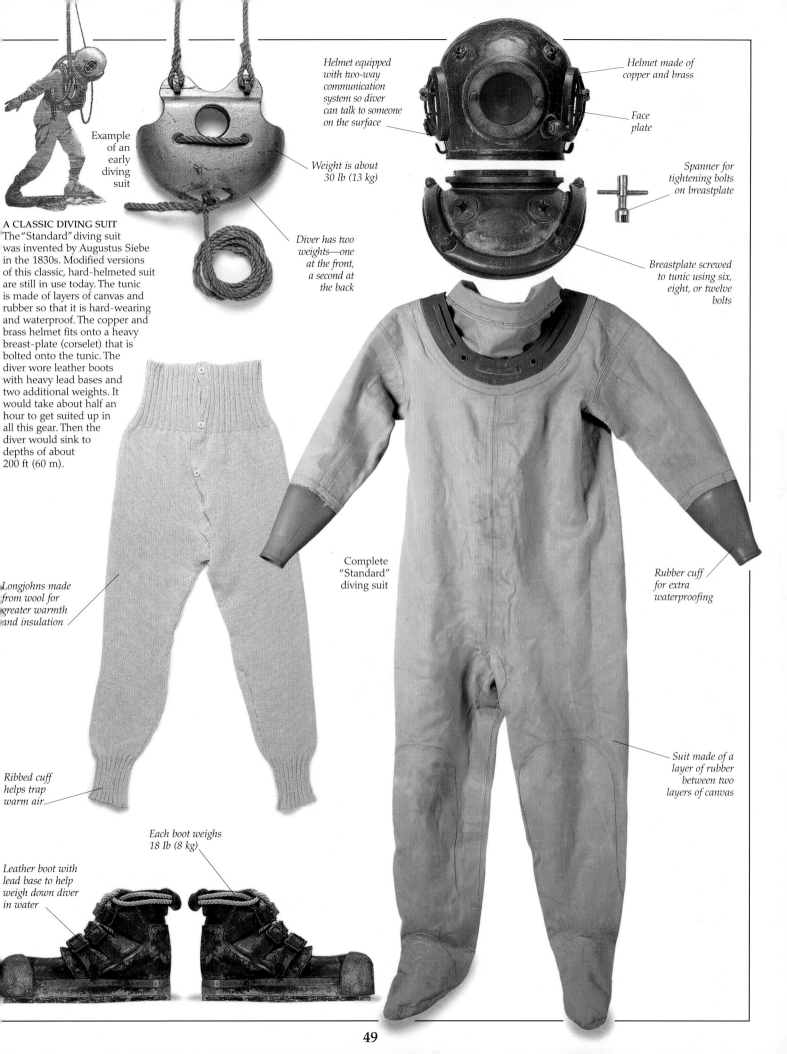

Example of an early diving suit

Helmet equipped with two-way communication system so diver can talk to someone on the surface

Helmet made of copper and brass

Face plate

Weight is about 30 lb (13 kg)

Spanner for tightening bolts on breastplate

A CLASSIC DIVING SUIT
The "Standard" diving suit was invented by Augustus Siebe in the 1830s. Modified versions of this classic, hard-helmeted suit are still in use today. The tunic is made of layers of canvas and rubber so that it is hard-wearing and waterproof. The copper and brass helmet fits onto a heavy breast-plate (corselet) that is bolted onto the tunic. The diver wore leather boots with heavy lead bases and two additional weights. It would take about half an hour to get suited up in all this gear. Then the diver would sink to depths of about 200 ft (60 m).

Diver has two weights—one at the front, a second at the back

Breastplate screwed to tunic using six, eight, or twelve bolts

Longjohns made from wool for greater warmth and insulation

Complete "Standard" diving suit

Rubber cuff for extra waterproofing

Ribbed cuff helps trap warm air

Suit made of a layer of rubber between two layers of canvas

Each boot weighs 18 lb (8 kg)

Leather boot with lead base to help weigh down diver in water

Underwater machines

Snort mast to renew and expel air with help of bellows

Augur for drilling into enemy ship to attach mine on rope

Vertical propeller

Delayed action mine

Side propeller powered by foot pedals

T**HE FIRST SUBMARINES** were simple designs. They allowed travel under water and were useful in war. More modern submarines were powered by diesel or gasoline while on the surface and used batteries under water. In 1955, the first submarine run on nuclear fuel traversed the oceans. Nuclear power allowed submarines to travel great distances before needing to refuel. Today, submarines have sophisticated sonar systems for navigating under water and pinpointing other vessels. They can carry high-powered torpedoes to fire at enemy craft or nuclear missiles. Submersibles (miniature submarines), used to explore the deep seafloor, cannot travel long distances. They need to be lowered from a support vessel on the surface.

"TURTLE" HERO
A one-man wooden submarine, the *Turtle*, was used during the Revolutionary War in 1776 to try to attach a delayed-action mine to an English ship blockading New York Harbor. The operator became disorientated by carbon dioxide building up inside the *Turtle*. He jettisoned the mine, which exploded harmlessly. Nevertheless, the explosion was enough to cause the British ship to up anchor and sail away.

External steering bar operated by diver

Internal steering position

Hand pump for pressurizing air reservoir and emptying ballast tanks

Front wheels smaller than back ones for easier turning

UNDERWATER ADVENTURE
Inspired by the invention of modern submarines, this 1900 engraving depicted a scene in the year 2000 with people enjoying a journey in a submarine liner. In a way, the prediction has come true as tourists can now take trips in small submarines to view marine life in places such as the Red Sea. However, most people explore the underwater world by learning to scuba dive or snorkel.

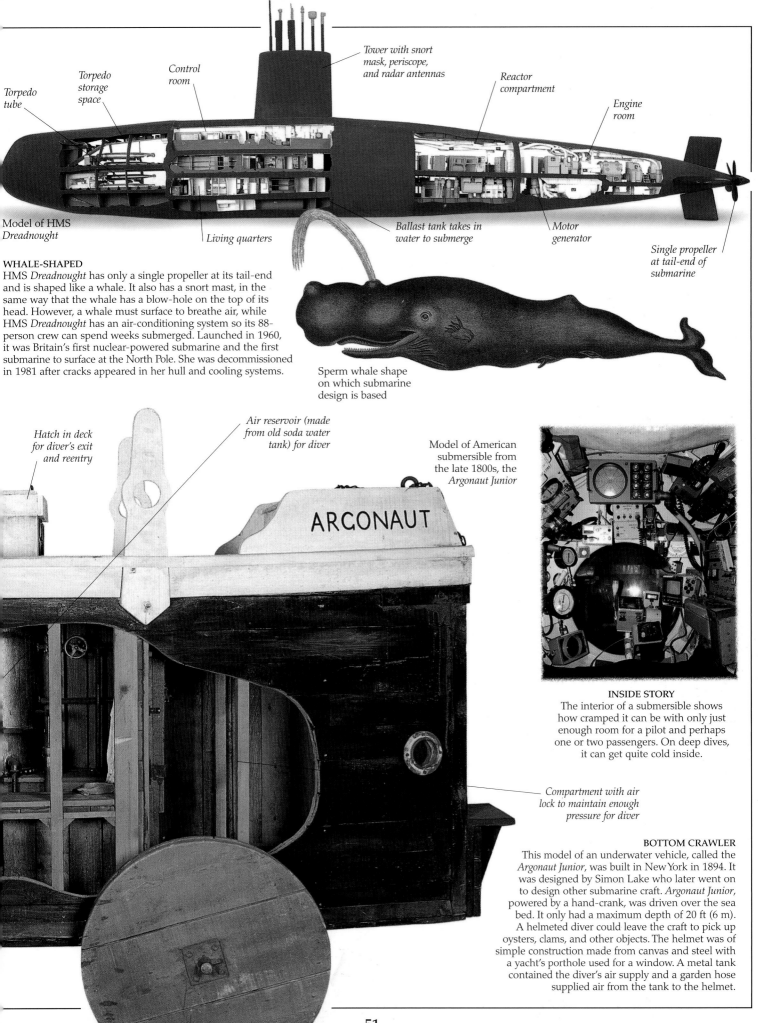

Torpedo tube

Torpedo storage space

Control room

Tower with snort mask, periscope, and radar antennas

Reactor compartment

Engine room

Model of HMS Dreadnought

Living quarters

Ballast tank takes in water to submerge

Motor generator

Single propeller at tail-end of submarine

WHALE-SHAPED

HMS *Dreadnought* has only a single propeller at its tail-end and is shaped like a whale. It also has a snort mast, in the same way that the whale has a blow-hole on the top of its head. However, a whale must surface to breathe air, while HMS *Dreadnought* has an air-conditioning system so its 88-person crew can spend weeks submerged. Launched in 1960, it was Britain's first nuclear-powered submarine and the first submarine to surface at the North Pole. She was decommissioned in 1981 after cracks appeared in her hull and cooling systems.

Sperm whale shape on which submarine design is based

Hatch in deck for diver's exit and reentry

Air reservoir (made from old soda water tank) for diver

Model of American submersible from the late 1800s, the *Argonaut Junior*

ARGONAUT

INSIDE STORY

The interior of a submersible shows how cramped it can be with only just enough room for a pilot and perhaps one or two passengers. On deep dives, it can get quite cold inside.

Compartment with air lock to maintain enough pressure for diver

BOTTOM CRAWLER

This model of an underwater vehicle, called the *Argonaut Junior*, was built in New York in 1894. It was designed by Simon Lake who later went on to design other submarine craft. *Argonaut Junior*, powered by a hand-crank, was driven over the sea bed. It only had a maximum depth of 20 ft (6 m). A helmeted diver could leave the craft to pick up oysters, clams, and other objects. The helmet was of simple construction made from canvas and steel with a yacht's porthole used for a window. A metal tank contained the diver's air supply and a garden hose supplied air from the tank to the helmet.

Ocean explorers

THE OCEAN HAS ALWAYS been a place of mystery, with little to see on the surface. The first depth soundings were made by simply dropping a lead weight on a line until the operator felt it hit the bottom. Echo sounders, invented during World War I, used single pulses of sound, which bounced back off the seabed. This led to increasingly sophisticated sonar systems, such as GLORIA. For centuries all that was known of marine life in the deep were creatures brought up in fishermen's nets or washed ashore. The HMS *Challenger* expedition of the 1870s undertook deep-sea trawls, finally showing that the deep ocean did contain marine life. The invention of manned submersibles allowed the deep-seafloor and its marine life to be directly observed. In the last 30 years startling new communities of animals have been discovered around hot springs on the ocean floor, while studies in shallow waters benefited greatly from the invention of SCUBA equipment (pp. 48–49). Today, unmanned submersibles have allowed further exploration in otherwise inaccessible waters. Yet, despite modern methods, who knows what mysteries the ocean still holds—for much of it is yet to be explored.

GLORIOUS GLORIA
GLORIA, for Geological Long Range Inclined Asdic (sonar), was used for over 20 years to survey the ocean floor, scanning over five percent of the world's oceans. GLORIA'S torpedo-shaped body (towfish) is 26 ft (8 m) long and weighs about 2 tons. On deck, GLORIA sat in a special cradle which was also used to launch the towfish into the water.

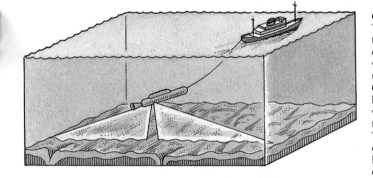

GLORIA AT WORK
To survey the seabed, GLORIA was towed behind its mother ship at a speed of 10 knots. Sound pulses from GLORIA would span out across the seabed up to 18 miles (30 km) on each side. GLORIA picked up echoes bouncing back from features on the seabed. These were processed by onboard computers to produce maps of the seafloor. These maps helped identify hazards on the seabed, determined routes for laying undersea cables, and assisted in exploration for valuable minerals.

Cradle's hydraulic system tipped GLORIA into the water

Inside GLORIA are two rows of transducers which emit sounds (sonar pulses)

Rope guide, used during recovery of GLORIA

Cable drum

GLORIA was towed by the nose

GLORIA covered up to 7,700 sq miles (20,000 sq km) in a day

Launching cradle weighs about 15 tons (13 metric tons)

Armored cable, 1,300 ft (400 m) long, contains electrical wiring for sending and receiving signals

SNORKELING

A simple way to observe life underwater is to snorkel. The snorkel goes under the strap of the face mask and sticks out above the water. By breathing in through the mouthpiece, air is drawn down the snorkel and air is expelled through the snorkel by breathing out.

Air expelled through end of snorkel

Fins propel swimmer along, but arms should be kept near the body for streamlining

Face mask traps air to let swimmer view life in the water

Diver looking at grouper fish in the Red Sea

Swimmer breathes in air and expels it through mouthpiece

Snorkel tube

SCUBA DIVING

Use of scuba equipment has proved invaluable in the study of marine life in shallow waters. Instead of bringing animals into an aquarium, marine biologists can observe them in the wild. Sometimes, animals such as hammerhead sharks are sensitive to the noises made by air bubbles and may be scared away.

DEEP STARS

Many different submersibles have been used for underwater exploration (right). The deepest dive ever was to 35,800 ft (10,912 m) in the Mariana Trench by the Swiss engineer Jacques Piccard and US Navy Lieutenant Don Walsh in their bathyscaphe in 1960.

Deep Star can reach depths of 4,000 ft (1,200 m)

PLANA

Fins used in snorkelling and SCUBA diving

AUTOSUB

This Autonomous Underwater Vehicle (AUV) is capable of exploring remote parts of the ocean. AUVs are unmanned and operate without being tethered to a ship or submersible. Since its launch in July 1996, Autosub has been used in over 300 projects, including missions beneath Antarctic sea ice.

Autosub uses a suite of sensors to collect data

Mechanical arm used to lower Autosub into the water

Wrecks on the seabed

Ever since people took to the sea in boats, there have been wrecks on the seabed. Mud and sand cover wooden boats, preserving them for centuries. This sediment protects the beams by keeping out the oxygen that speeds up decay. Metal-hulled ships are badly corroded by seawater. The *Titanic*'s steel hull could disintegrate within a hundred years. Wrecks in shallow water get covered by plant and animal life, turning them into living reefs. Aside from animals, such as corals and sponges growing on the outside, fish shelter inside as if in an underwater cave. Wrecks and their objects tell us much about life in the past, but archeologists must first survey them carefully. Objects brought up are washed clean of salt and sometimes treated with chemicals to preserve them. Treasure seekers, unfortunately, can do much damage.

Less valuable silver coin

GLITTERING GOLD
Gold is among the most sought-after treasure. These Spanish coins, much in demand by pirates, sometimes ended up on the seabed when a ship sank.

Sonar equipment

Titanium sphere protects passengers

IFREM
DCN CE

SUPER SUB
The French submersible, *Nautile*, recovered objects from the seabed surrounding the wreck of the *Titanic*. When the ship went down, it broke in two, scattering objects far and wide. Only a submersible could dive deep enough to reach the *Titanic*, 2.5 miles (3,780 m) down. With space for only three people (pilot, copilot, and an observer), they sit in a sphere made of titanium metal, which protects them from the immense pressure at these depths. Extrathick, curved plexiglass portholes become flat on a dive due to pressure. The journey to the wreck takes about an hour and a half, and *Nautile* can stay down for eight hours.

Lights for video camera

Manipulator arm for picking objects off seabed

VALUABLE PROPERTY
In 1892, divers worked on the wreck of the tug *L'Abeille*, which sank off Le Havre, France. For centuries, people have salvaged wrecks to bring up items of value.

SAD REMINDERS
Many items recovered from the *Titanic* wreck were not valuable, but everyday items used by those aboard. Personal effects, such as buttons or just cutlery, remind us of those who died.

THE UNSINKABLE SHIP
In 1912, the *Titanic* sailed from England to New York on her maiden voyage. Because of her hull's watertight compartments, she was thought unsinkable, but hit an iceberg four days into the voyage. She took two hours and forty minutes to sink, with only 705 people saved out of 2,228. She was discovered in 1985 by a French-US team, using remote-controlled video equipment. The submersibles *Alvin* (US) and *Mir* (Russia) have also dived to the wreck since then.

PLANE WRECK

Airplanes sometimes crash into the sea and sink to the bottom, like this Japanese biplane discovered off Papua New Guinea in the Pacific. The Bermuda Triangle, an area in the Atlantic, was famous for the many planes and ships which mysteriously disappeared there.

SUNKEN TREASURE

These precious jewels are among many valuable items salvaged from the wreck of the Spanish galleon, the *Tolossa*, in the 1970s. Bound for Mexico in 1724, she foundered on a massive coral reef during a hurricane. Many luxury goods were recovered from the wreck, which show that the Spanish were exporting fine things to their New World colonies during the 1700s. Other items from the wreck include brass guns, iron grenades, and hundreds of pearls.

Gold, diamonds, and pearls salvaged from the wreck of the Tolossa *off Hispaniola*

Nautile measures 26 ft 6 in (8 m) in length

Thruster provides the power for forward movement

Encrusted Roman jar

Barnacle

Mollusk shell

MISSING LAND

This poster advertises a film about the lost continent of Atlantis, which supposedly sunk beneath the sea. This myth may be true, since a Greek island sank beneath the waves after an earthquake in c. 1600 BCE.

HOME, SWEET HOME

Hard barnacle shells and tubes of worms grew on this Roman jar while it rested for hundreds of years on the seabed. Animals that normally live on rocks are just as happy to settle on any hard objects left in the sea, such as shipwrecks, but some animal growths are hard to remove without damaging objects.

Worm tube

Harvesting fish

FISH ARE THE MOST popular kind of seafood, with some 77 million tons (70 million metric tons) caught around the world each year. Some fish are caught by hand-thrown nets and traps in local waters, but far more are caught at sea by modern fishing vessels using the latest technology. Some fish are caught on long lines with many hooks or ensnared when they swim into long walls of drift nets. Bottom-dwelling fish are trawled or whole shoals are gathered up in huge nets set in midwater. Using sonar to detect shoals means there are few places where fish can escape notice. Even fish living in deep waters, such as orange roughy at depths of 3,300 ft (1,000 m), are brought up in numbers. Many people are concerned that too many fish are being caught because numbers take a long time to recover. Competition for fish stocks is fierce and it is difficult for fishermen to make a living. But some fish, such as salmon, are farmed to help meet demand.

1 HATCHING OUT Salmon begin life in rivers and streams where they hatch from eggs laid in a shallow hollow among gravel. First the fry (alevins) grow, using the contents of their egg sac attached to their bellies as food.

2 YOUNG SALMON At a few weeks old, the egg sac disappears, so young salmon must feed on tiny insects in the river. Soon dark spots appear on the young salmon (called parr). The parr stay in the river for a year or more, before turning into silvery smolt which head for the sea.

Fin rays are well-developed

Large, first dorsal fin

3 AT SEA Atlantic salmon spend up to four years at sea, feeding on other fishes. They grow rapidly, putting on several pounds annually. Then the mature salmon return to their home rivers and streams where they hatch. They recognize their home stream by a number of clues, including its "smell" (particular combinations of tiny quantities of substances in the water).

Pelvic fin

Pectoral fin

Operculum (flap covering gills)

Mouth for feeding and taking in water to "breathe"

FISH FARMING Salmon are among the few kinds of sea fish to be farmed successfully. Young salmon are reared in freshwater then, when large enough, released into floating pens in calm sea waters, such as sea lochs. To help them grow quickly, the salmon are fed with dried fish pellets. Environmentalists are concerned that fish parasites, called sea lice, common among farmed salmon, are infecting and killing wild salmon. Biologists are investigating ways to combat this problem.

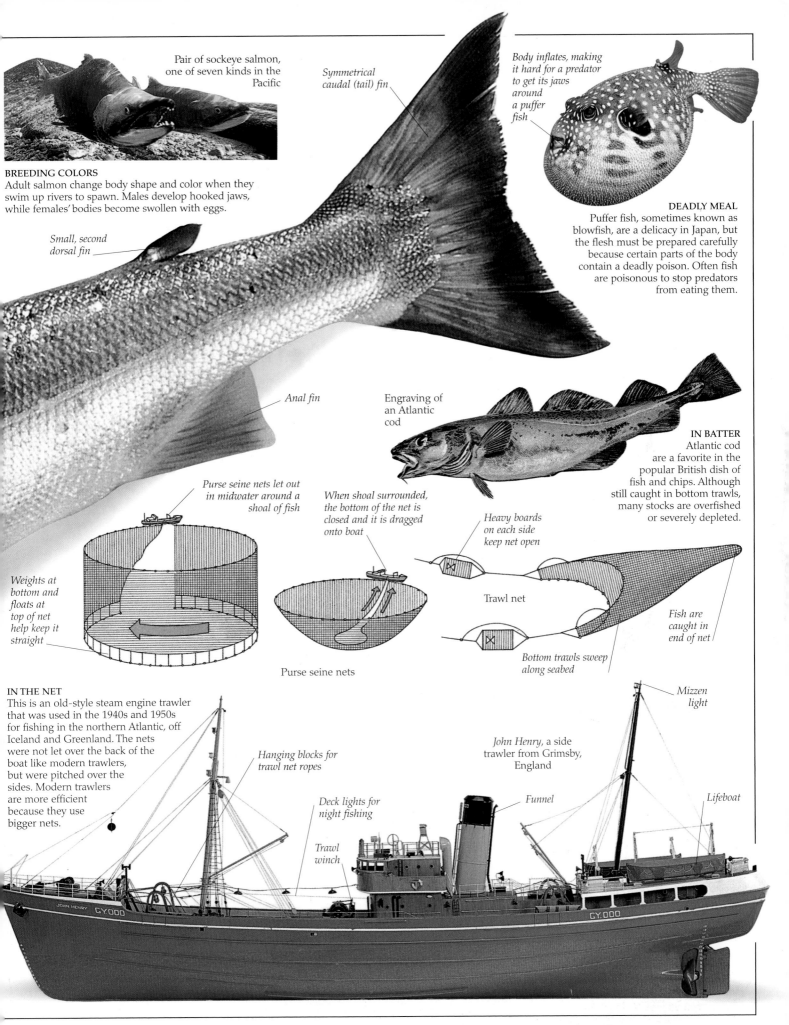

Pair of sockeye salmon, one of seven kinds in the Pacific

Symmetrical caudal (tail) fin

Body inflates, making it hard for a predator to get its jaws around a puffer fish

BREEDING COLORS
Adult salmon change body shape and color when they swim up rivers to spawn. Males develop hooked jaws, while females' bodies become swollen with eggs.

Small, second dorsal fin

DEADLY MEAL
Puffer fish, sometimes known as blowfish, are a delicacy in Japan, but the flesh must be prepared carefully because certain parts of the body contain a deadly poison. Often fish are poisonous to stop predators from eating them.

Anal fin

Engraving of an Atlantic cod

IN BATTER
Atlantic cod are a favorite in the popular British dish of fish and chips. Although still caught in bottom trawls, many stocks are overfished or severely depleted.

Purse seine nets let out in midwater around a shoal of fish

When shoal surrounded, the bottom of the net is closed and it is dragged onto boat

Heavy boards on each side keep net open

Weights at bottom and floats at top of net help keep it straight

Trawl net

Fish are caught in end of net

Bottom trawls sweep along seabed

Purse seine nets

IN THE NET
This is an old-style steam engine trawler that was used in the 1940s and 1950s for fishing in the northern Atlantic, off Iceland and Greenland. The nets were not let over the back of the boat like modern trawlers, but were pitched over the sides. Modern trawlers are more efficient because they use bigger nets.

Hanging blocks for trawl net ropes

Mizzen light

John Henry, a side trawler from Grimsby, England

Deck lights for night fishing

Funnel

Lifeboat

Trawl winch

JOHN HENRY GY.000

GY.000

Ocean products

PEOPLE HAVE ALWAYS HARVESTED plants and animals from the ocean. Many different animals are collected for food, from fish, crustaceans (shrimps, lobsters), and mollusks (clams, squid) to more unusual foods, such as sea cucumbers, barnacles, and jellyfish. Seaweeds are eaten, too, either in a recognizable state or as an ingredient of ice creams and other processed foods. The products made from sea creatures are amazing, although many (such as mother-of-pearl buttons and sponges) now are replaced by synthetic materials. Yet the appeal of natural ocean products is so great that some sea animals and certain kinds of seaweeds are cultivated. Among sea creatures to be farmed are giant clams (for pretty shells), mussels (for food), and pearl oysters. Farming is one way to meet demand for products, and to avoid overcollecting the ocean's wildlife.

Yarn dyed purple from pigment of sea snails

ROYAL PURPLE
Sea snails were used to make purple dye for clothes worn by kings in ancient times. Making dye was a smelly process, as huge quantities of salted snails were left in vats gouged out of rocks. The purple liquid was collected and heated to concentrate the dye. These sea snails (from Florida and the Caribbean) are used to make purple dye.

Slate-pencil sea urchin from tropical coral reefs in the Indo-Pacific

Short, blunt spines surround mouth

USEFUL SPINES
The spines of this urchin were once used as pencils to write on slate boards. Slate-pencil urchins are still collected, their spines used for wind chimes. Hung from threads, the spines clink together when the wind blows through them. Urchins use their big spines to help them walk across the seabed, when they emerge from crevices to feed at night.

Long, very strong spines help protect urchin from predators

Spines help urchin move and to hold it in place

Five, strong white teeth protrude from urchin's mouth (viewed from underneath)

Soft skeleton left after processing living sponge

SOFT SKELETON
Bath sponges, harvested from the sandy seabed, grow among sea grasses in reef lagoons. When brought up from the bottom, the sponges are covered with slimy, living tissues. Mainly collected from the Mediterranean, Caribbean, and Pacific, natural sponges are prone to diseases and overcollecting.

SEAWEED FARM
In Japan, seaweeds are used in crackers and to wrap raw fish parcels. Red seaweed is grown in the sea on bamboo poles, collected, and dried. Laver, a similar kind of red seaweed, is eaten in Wales, UK. Made from red seaweeds, agar (a jellylike substance) is used in foods and in medical research. Seaweeds are also used as fertilizers.

SHINY PEARLS

Pearls are produced by mussels and oysters in response to irritation. Natural pearls form around a piece of grit that gets between the oyster's shell and its skin (mantle). Tissues from the mantle surround the grit to produce mother-of-pearl layers. Pearls are cultivated by inserting particles into a clam, along with some skin from another clam. Many kinds of clams produce pearls, but only those with shiny, inner layers to the shell make shiny pearls.

Double strand of blue pearls

SALT PANS

When seawater evaporates, a salt-crystal crust is left behind. Large quantities of sea salt are produced by flooding shallow ponds (pans) with seawater and letting the water evaporate in the hot sun. Sea salt is produced in places with warm weather and little rain. The salt in seawater is mostly sodium chloride, but there is also sulphate, magnesium, calcium, and potassium.

Shell can close to protect itself from predators

Gloves can be made from byssus threads of noble pen shell

Noble pen shell grows to 2 ft (60 cm) in length

Tapered shell is brittle

Silver cross inlaid with abalone shell

Hole to expel water and waste

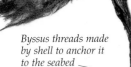

Byssus threads made by shell to anchor it to the seabed

GOLDEN THREADS

The pen shell produces a thick mat of byssus threads to anchor it in the soft seabed of the Mediterranean. These threads were once collected, spun into fine, golden thread, and then woven into cloth. Some say the cloth may have started the legend of the golden fleece of Ancient Greek mythology, where the fleece was that of a winged ram.

RAINBOW HUES

Inside an abalone shell are all the colors of the rainbow. The heavy shell's mother-of-pearl is used to make jewellery and buttons. These shells are popular with New Zealand's Maoris. Abalones are also eaten. With a muscular foot that clings to the seabed, the shells have to be prised off the bottom.

Oil and gas exploration

Vᴀʟᴜᴀʙʟᴇ ʀᴇꜱᴇʀᴠᴏɪʀꜱ ᴏꜰ ᴏɪʟ ᴀɴᴅ ɢᴀꜱ lie hidden in rocks beneath the seabed. Oil and gas are tapped by drilling down through the rocks, but first geologists must know where to drill. Only certain kinds of rocks hold oil and gas, but must be in shallow enough water to be reached by drilling. Geologists find the reservoirs by sending shock waves through the seabed and using the returning signals to distinguish between the rock layers. Temporary rigs are set up to pinpoint a source to see if the oil is the right quality and quantity. To extract oil or gas, the rig is replaced by a more permanent oil platform, which is firmly anchored to the seabed. Oil can be piped ashore or processed and stored on floating vessels (FPSOs) until it is offloaded onto tankers. When reservoirs dry up, new sources have to be found as there is a great demand for energy, but the Earth's supplies of oil and gas are limited. The main offshore oil fields are in the North Sea, Gulf of Mexico, Persian Gulf, and along the coasts of South America and Asia.

WIND TURBINES
Unlike oil, wind turbines are a source of renewable energy. Some thirty turbines operate at North Hoyle Offshore Wind Farm, located 6 miles (10 km) off Rhyl in North Wales, UK.

Tallest structure on this platform is flare stack for safety reasons

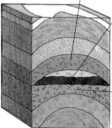

Impermeable rock prevents oil from traveling through

Oil is trapped in porous, reservoir rock

Porous rock that oil can pass through

DEATH AND DECAY
Plant and bacteria remains from ancient seas fell to the sea floor and were covered by mud layers. Heat and pressure turned them into oil, then gas, which moved up through porous rocks, to be trapped by impermeable rocks.

AT WORK
On a drilling platform, workers are looking after the drill bit that is used to cut down through the rocks on the seabed. When in operation, special mud is sent down pipes attached to the drill bit to cool it, wash out the ground-up rock and prevent the oil from gushing out.

ON FIRE
Oil and gas are highly flammable. Despite precautions, accidents do happen, like the North Sea's *Piper Alpha* disaster in 1988 when 167 people died. Since then safety measures have been improved.

FLOATING PRODUCTION
The oil industry increasingly uses floating vessels called FPSOs (Floating Production, Storage, Offloading). These vessels take the oil and gas produced from nearby drilling platforms and undersea wells. The FPSO processes the oil and stores it, until it is taken away by tankers. FPSOs work well in deepwater locations which are too far to connect to the shore by seabed pipelines. The vessels can also move out of the way of hurricanes or drifting icebergs. They can also move when an oil field is exhausted.

FPSO GIRASSOL

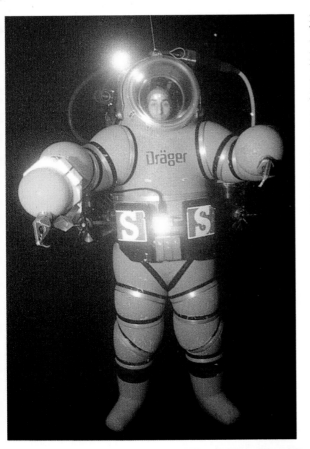

NEWT SUIT
Thick-walled suits, like the one above, resist pressure. When under water, the diver breathes air at normal pressure as if inside a submersible. This means a diver can go deeper without having to undergo decompression (p. 48). Newt suits (above) are used in oil exploration to depths of 1,200 ft (365 m). Joints in the arms and legs allow the diver to move.

MILK ROUND
Helicopters deliver supplies to oil platforms far out at sea. Up to 400 people can live and work on an oil platform. Crew includes geologists who examine the rocks, oil and gas samples, mechanics to look after the machinery, and cooks to feed the crew.

ON THE BOTTOM
Divers (minus Newt suits), doing repairs under water, work longer if they return to a pressurized chamber, then back into the sea, without having to decompress after each dive.

Helicopter pad—fresh food and milk are flown in

Living quarters

Fireproof lifeboat gives better chance of survival

Strong structure to withstand buffeting by wind and waves

DANGER UNDERWATER HAZARD

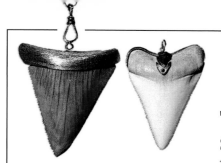

Jewelry made of teeth of the great white shark, now protected in some areas

Oceans in peril

THE OCEANS AND THE LIFE THEY SUPPORT are under threat. Sewage and industrial waste are dumped into the oceans and poured from pipelines, carrying with them certain chemicals that can create a dangerous buildup in the food chain. Oil spills smother and poison marine life.

Cut to show mother-of-pearl

Garbagge dumped at sea can choke a turtle or trap a seabird. Many seabirds and sea mammals drown when caught in abandoned fishing nets. Overharvesting has depleted many ocean animals, from whales to fish. Even the souvenir trade threatens coral reefs. However, the situation is improving. Now, laws help stop ocean pollution, regulations protect marine life, and in underwater parks people can look at ocean life, but not disturb it.

HAVE A HEART
Many people collect sea shells, because of their beauty, but most shells sold in stores have been taken as living animals, so if too many shelled creatures are collected from one place, such as a coral reef, the pattern of life can be disrupted. Shells should only be bought if the harvest is properly managed. It is better to go beachcombing and collect shells of already dead creatures. Always check about taking even empty shells, since some nature reserves do not permit this.

Heart cockle shells

OIL SPILL
Oil is needed for industry and vehicles. Huge quantities are transported at sea in tankers, sent along pipelines, and brought up from the seabed. Accidents happen where massive amounts of oil are spilled. Seabirds and sea mammals die of the cold, because their feathers or fur no longer contain pockets of air to keep them warm. Trying to clean themselves, animals die from consuming the oil, which can block their airways. Some are rescued, cleaned, and released back into the wild.

SAVING BEAUTY
No one can help but admire this beautifully crafted, 17th-century, chambered nautilus shell. There are six kinds of nautilus living in the Pacific and Indian Oceans today, where they are at risk from overcollecting. They are easily hunted at night when they rise to the surface. Empty shells are collected because they can also float at the surface. Chambered nautili grow quite slowly, reaching maturity in six or more years, so if too many are collected the populations can take a long time to recover.

WORSE FOR WHALES

For centuries, whales have been hunted for their meat, oil, and bones. Whale oil was used in foods, as lubricants, and in soap and candles, and the broad baleen plates were made into household items such as brushes. The wholesale slaughter by commercial whalers drastically reduced the number of whales. Now most whales are protected, but scientists doubt whether some populations will ever recover their former numbers. Some kinds of whales are still caught for food, mainly by local people.

Japanese painting showing early whalers in small boats risking their lives in pursuit of whales

Oily whale meat extract used to make margarine

Ground-up whale meal used in animal feed and pet food

Whale liver oil was a source of vitamin A

Sperm oil was a high-grade lubricant for motors and cars

Engraved nautilus shell

Intricate floral pattern cut into shell

Sponges settled on scrap iron in a Red Sea harbor

TAKE CARE

A basket sponge this size may be 100 years old, but could be damaged in an instant by a diver's thoughtless kick. Many kinds of sea life are more fragile than they look. Corals can be killed if touched by divers. All kinds of junk end up on the seabed (center right) and can smother marine life. Air pollution can also affect sea life. During the 1997–98 El Niño, sea temperatures rose by 2–4°F (1–2°C) in many parts of the Indian Ocean, causing some corals to eject their algae partners and die. Many scientists suspect global warming may have contributed to the unusual temperature rise.

Did you know?

FASCINATING FACTS

⭐ The world's oceans contain 97% of all the Earth's water. Of the remaining 3%, just over 2% is locked in ice, and just under 1% is freshwater (in streams, rivers, lakes, and in the ground) and water vapor.

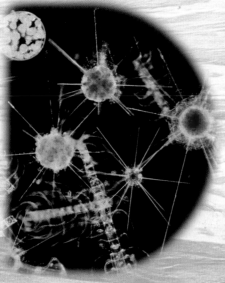

Earth seen from space

⭐ From above the Pacific Ocean, in space, the planet looks almost entirely blue. In fact, the Pacific Ocean, at 59 million sq miles (153 million sq km) covers about one third of the Earth's surface.

Plankton magnified several hundred times

⭐ The coldest sea surface temperature is in the White Sea, in the Arctic Ocean, at 28.4°F (−2°C). The warmest occurs in summer in shallow parts of the Indian Ocean's Persian Gulf, at 96.1°F (35.6°C).

⭐ The temperature of the oceans' deepest water is between 34–39°F (2 and 4°C).

⭐ The highest underwater mountain is in the Pacific Ocean, near New Zealand. At 5.4 miles (8.7 km) tall, it is nearly as high as Mount Everest, the world's highest mountain.

⭐ The greatest tidal range and the highest tides in the world occur in Canada's Bay of Fundy, in the Atlantic, where the difference between low and high tides can be up to 52 ft (16 m).

⭐ Ninety percent of all marine life occurs in the sunlit, or euphotic, zone—the surface layer of the ocean where there is enough light to support photosynthesis. Plankton (free-floating aquatic organisms) float here, providing the basis of the ocean's food chain.

⭐ A bucket of seawater can contain up to 10 million phytoplankton (single-celled microscopic ocean plants) and zooplankton (microscopic animals). Most phytoplankton are less than 0.01 mm wide.

⭐ The largest meat-eating fish is the great white shark. Some adults can grow up to 20 ft (6 m) long and weigh around 1.5 tons.

⭐ A great white shark can detect one part of blood from a wounded animal in 100 million parts of water.

⭐ Flying fish can leap up to 6 ft (2 m) out of the water to escape from such predators as sailfish and marlins.

⭐ Once airborne, a flying fish spreads out the fins on its chest so they act like wings and can "fly" 325 ft (100 m).

Tiny cleaner wrasse at work inside the mouth of a grouper fish

⭐ At birth, a baby blue whale can weigh about 3 tons. The babies guzzle 50 gallons (100 liters) of their mother's milk a day and grow at a rate of almost 11 lbs (5 kg) an hour.

⭐ Small fish called cleaner wrasse feed on parasites that infest much larger fish, such as a grouper, even swimming right inside the larger fish's mouth to feed. Bigger fish do not harm the wrasse; sometimes they even form lines at the wrasses' "cleaning station" to divest themselves of parasites.

Spines flattened against body   Porcupine fish at its normal size…

Body spines stick out   … and when inflated

⭐ If threatened, a porcupine fish takes in water to swell its body to twice its normal size, making it too large and uncomfortable to swallow. The fish slowly returns to its normal size when the danger has passed.

QUESTIONS AND ANSWERS

Q Why is the sea salty?

A The sea's salinity comes from salt washed out of the Earth's rock, sand, and soils by rainwater then carried in streams and rivers to the sea. This has been happening for millions of years, building up the sea's concentration of salt. Sodium chloride, or common salt (the kind we put on our food), makes up around 85% of the minerals in the sea.

Waves forming out at sea

Q What causes waves?

A Most waves are created by the wind blowing across the open ocean and causing the surface water to ripple. If the wind continues to blow, the ripples grow larger and turn into waves. The height of waves depends on the strength and duration of the wind causing them and how far they have been "pushed" across the ocean.

Q Why is the sea blue?

A Blue light from sunlight (which is made up of all the colors of the rainbow) is the least absorbed by clear seawater. When sunlight enters the water, the blue light is scattered and some is reflected back to the surface, making the sea look blue.

Q How many types of fish are there?

A There are around 25,000 different species of marine and freshwater fish. Of this number, around 24,000 are bony fish, 1,100 are cartilaginous or gristly fish (such as sharks and rays), and about 100 are hagfish and lampreys—the so-called jawless fishes.

Larger upper tail vane

Tail vanes equal in size

Cartilaginous fish—blacktip reef shark (top) and bony fish—mackerel (above)

Q What is the difference between bony and cartilaginous fish?

A As their name suggests, bony fish have bony skeletons whereas sharks and rays have skeletons made of cartilage (gristle). In addition, a bony fish has a gas-filled swim bladder to control buoyancy. This can be adjusted to make the fish weightless in water so it can rest or remain motionless. Gristly fish, however, will visually sink if they don't keep moving. Other characteristic differences are that bony fish have tail vanes of equal size and protective gill flaps, whereas most sharks have larger upper tail vanes than lower ones, and gill slits without flaps.

Stargazer hiding in gravel on the seabed

Q How do fish hide from predators in the open sea?

A Many fish that live near the sea's surface have dark backs and paler underbellies. This countershading camouflages them from above and below. Fish that live on the seabed are often colored and patterned to blend in with their surroundings.

Record Breakers

★ **LARGEST SEA CREATURE**
The blue whale is the world's largest animal, at up to 100 ft (30 m) long and as much as 165 tons (150 metric tons) in weight.

★ **BIGGEST FISH**
The whale shark can grow up to 42 ft (12.5 m) long and weigh up to 22 tons (20 metric tons).

★ **SMALLEST FISH**
The adult Marshall Islands dwarf goby is just ⅓ in (6 mm) from nose to tail.

★ **HEAVIEST BONY FISH**
The ocean sunfish, or *Mala mola*, can weigh up to 2 tons.

★ **FASTEST FISH**
The sailfish can reach speeds of up to 68 mph (109 km/h)—faster than a cheetah can run.

Whale shark

The world's oceans

THERE ARE FIVE OCEANS—THE PACIFIC, ATLANTIC, INDIAN, ARCTIC, AND SOUTHERN. The first four fill natural basins in the Earth's crust. The Southern Ocean is technically part of the southern Pacific, Atlantic, and Indian Oceans but was officially delimited from them in 2000 south of 60 degrees latitude, by the International Hydrographic Organization. This coincides with the limits of the Antarctic Treaty.

PACIFIC OCEAN

The Pacific Ocean is the world's largest ocean, covering about 28% of the Earth's surface. The ocean has between 20,000 and 30,000 islands, and is surrounded by a "Ring of Fire," where the Earth's tectonic plates are sliding into ocean trenches, causing volcanic activity and frequent earthquakes.

AREA: 58,957,258 sq miles (152,617,160 sq km)
Includes: Bali Sea, Bering Sea, Bering Strait, Coral Sea, East China Sea, Florest Sea, Gulf of Alaska, Gulf of Tonkin, Java Sea, Philippine Sea, Savu Sea, Sea of Japan, Sea of Okhotsk, South China Sea, Tasman Sea, Timor Sea
AVERAGE DEPTH: 13,874 ft (4,229 m)
DEEPEST POINT: 36,201 ft (11,034 m) Challenger Deep in the Mariana Trench
COASTLINE: 84,299 miles (135,663 km)
CLIMATE: Strong currents and trade winds constantly blow across the Pacific's waters, affecting its climate and weather

Kaiko submersible

and often causing violent tropical storms. A cold current usually flows from the western coast of South America. However, every few years a warm current (El Niño) flows east toward Peru, causing worldwide weather changes.

Unmanned sub reached bottom of the Mariana Trench in 1995

NATURAL RESOURCES: Fish stocks, oil, and gas fields, sand, and gravel aggregates.

Coral atoll reef in the southwest Pacific

ENVIRONMENTAL ISSUES: Nearly half of the world's shipping routes cross the Pacific, including huge supertankers, giant bulk carriers and container ships. As a result, the ocean suffers from oil pollution, especially in the Philippine Sea and the South China Sea, which threatens marine life and seabirds. Some of the Pacific's endangered marine creatures include dugongs, sea otters, sea lions, seals, turtles, and whales.

ATLANTIC OCEAN

The Atlantic Ocean is the world's second-largest ocean, covering about one-fifth of the Earth's surface. An underwater mountain chain called the Mid-Atlantic Ridge runs down its center.

Panama Canal links the Atlantic and Pacific

AREA: 31,563,463 sq miles (81,527,400 sq km)
Includes: Baltic Sea, Black Sea, Caribbean Sea, Davis Strait, Denmark Strait, Gulf of Guinea, Gulf of Mexico, Labrador Sea, Mediterranean Sea, North Sea, Norwegian Sea, Sargasso Sea, Scotia Sea
AVERAGE DEPTH: 12,391 ft (3,777 m)
DEEPEST POINT: 28,232 ft (8,605 m) Milwaukee Deep in the Puerto Rico Trench
COASTLINES: 69,512 miles (111,866 km)
CLIMATE: The Atlantic's northerly waters are usually covered with sea ice in the northern winter, and huge icebergs drifting southwards are sometimes a problem to shipping from February to August. The Gulf Stream, a warm water current, flows from the Gulf of Mexico, north and then east, feeding the North Atlantic Drift, which raises the temperatures of northern Europe and keeps many northern ports ice-free during the winter.

NATURAL RESOURCES: Fish, oil, and gas fields, sand, and gravel aggregates.
ENVIRONMENT ISSUES: Some Atlantic waters are polluted from industrial waste, sewage, and oil. Fish stocks have run low because of overfishing, especially through trawling for bottom-dwelling fish such as cod.

Atlantic fishing trawler

INDIAN OCEAN

The Indian Ocean is the world's third-largest ocean. Its northern ocean currents change direction according to the monsoon winds, flowing southwest along the coast of Somalia in the northern winter and the opposite direction in the northern summer.

Endangered green turtle

AREA: 26,064,036 sq miles (67,469,536 sq km)
Includes: Andaman Sea, Arabian Sea, Bay of Bengal, Great Australian Bight, Gulf of Aden, Gulf of Oman, Java Sea, Mozambique Channel, Persian Gulf, Red Sea, Timor Sea, Strait of Malacca
AVERAGE DEPTH: 12,720 ft (3,877 m)
DEEPEST POINT: 23,376 ft (7,125 m) Java Trench
COASTLINE: 41,338 miles (66,526 km)
CLIMATE: Cool, dry winds blow over the ocean from the northeast between February and March. Between August and September, the wind changes direction and southwesterly winds blow north from the ocean, bringing heavy monsoon rain and flooding to coastal regions.

NATURAL RESOURCES: Oil and gas fields, sand and gravel, fish.
ENVIRONMENTAL ISSUES: Oil pollution in the Arabian Sea, Persian Gulf and Red Sea; endangered sea creatures include the dugong, turtles, and whales.

Oil production in the Arabian Sea

ARCTIC OCEAN

The Arctic Ocean is the world's smallest ocean. Between December and May, most of the ocean is covered by polar ice, which can be up to 100 ft (30 m) thick.

AREA: (3,351,811 sq miles (8,676,520 sq km)
Includes: Baffin Bay, Barents Sea, Beaufort Sea, Chukchi Sea, East Siberian Sea, Greenland Sea, Hudson Bay, Hudson Straight, Kara Sea, Laptev Sea, and the Northwest Passage
AVERAGE DEPTH: 6,349 ft (1,935 m)
DEEPEST POINT: 18,400 ft (5,680 m) Fram Basin
COASTLINE: 28,204 miles (45,389 km)
CLIMATE: Polar, with continuous cold and narrow annual temperature ranges.

Ice breakers have thick steel hulls to crush ice and open up a lane for other ships

NATURAL RESOURCES: Oil and gas fields, sand and gravel aggregates, fish, and marine mammals.
ENVIRONMENTAL ISSUES: The extent of the sea ice is diminishing due to climate change creating problems for many marine animals. As the ice melts earlier, polar bears have less time to hunt for seals on the ice.

Polar bear

Partly webbed front paws for swimming

SOUTHERN OCEAN

The Southern Ocean is the world's fourth-largest ocean. Parts of the ocean freeze in the southern winter, forming the vast Ronne and Ross ice shelves. Currents beneath the ice shelves cause giant slabs of ice to break away, which melt as they float northwards.

AREA: 8,102,165 sq miles (20,973,318 sq km)
Includes: Amundsen Sea, Bellingshausen Sea, Ross Sea, Weddell Sea

AVERAGE DEPTH: 14,760 ft (4,500 m)
DEEPEST POINT: 23,737 ft (7,235 m) South Sandwich Trench
COASTLINE: 11,165 miles (17,968 km)
CLIMATE: Polar, with continuous cold and narrow annual temperature ranges.
NATURAL RESOURCES: Probable large oil and gas fields, sand and gravel aggregates, fish, krill.

ENVIRONMENTAL ISSUES: Ultraviolet radiation penetrating through the ozone hole above the Antarctic is damaging phytoplankton. Although protected by the 1959 Antarctic Treaty and subsequent annexes, some illegal and unregulated fishing still occurs. However, protected whale and fur seal populations are making a comeback after overexploitation in the 18th and 19th centuries.

Characteristic flat-topped Antarctic iceberg

Statistics compiled from data from the Naval Oceanographic Office, Stennis Space Center, Mississippi (2001)

Find out more

THERE IS A WEALTH OF INFORMATION available about the oceans and marine life—so it is easy to find out more about them even if you do not live (or go on vacation) near the sea. The first stop should be an aquarium. Many have impressive exhibits of sea creatures displayed in their natural settings, so you can see the inhabitants of a coral reef, a mangrove, or the open ocean up close. Watch, also, for excellent wildlife programs on television, or search the Internet using the Web sites listed below as a starting point.

Razor shell encrusted with barnacles, oyster (behind) and slipper limpet

SEA SHELLS
If you visit the beach, look for seashells washed up on the shore. Take along a guidebook to help you identify them. Always put inhabited shells back where you find them, however, and never collect shells from a protected site. Many reefs, such as Australia's Great Barrier Reef, are conservation zones, and removing shells can damage the ecosystem.

VISIT AN AQUARIUM
Plan a visit to an aquarium to observe a huge range of marine life from all over the world's oceans. Many large aquariums have impressive viewing tanks containing hundreds of species, from jellyfish and giant octopuses to sharks and starfish. Some tanks are spread over several levels; others have transparent tunnels so you can walk right underneath the water. Watch for special events when you can get up close to sharks, rays, and other marine creatures.

USEFUL WEBSITES

- Join research scientists on an underwater exploration: **www.at-sea.org**
- Visit the coastal Louisiana site for quizzes, tips on identifying birds, and a coloring book: **www.lacoast.gov/education/kids**
- Download your own tidepool flashcards, as well as printouts on ocean topics for grades K–12: **www.mms.gov/mmskids**
- Homepage of Monterey Bay Aquarium with web cams: **www.mbayaq.org/**

STUDY A TIDE POOL
Tide pools are filled with a wide variety of plants and animals. Even if you visit the same pool several times, it is unlikely you will find the same creatures, making these habitats endlessly fascinating, dynamic environments to study. Look for starfish, anemones, mussels, and seaweed such as sea lettuce and kelp. If you stand very still, you may also spot crabs hiding in crevices between rocks, or a tiny fish.

Places to visit

Pewter pitcher from the *Mary Rose*

FACE TO FACE

You can see marine life close up if you take a trip in a glass-bottomed boat or a tourist submarine. Or try snorkeling—it's amazing what you can see once you're below the ocean's surface, especially if you snorkel over a coral reef; but don't touch anything—especially sponges or coral—because you may damage or even kill it.

Flukes (tail parts) of a humpback whale

WHALE WATCHING

Various companies, especially in Canada and the United States, organize whale-watching vacations, giving you the chance of seeing whales in their natural environment. The tourists pictured left are observing humpback whales off the coast of Alaska.

MARINE SANCTUARIES

Marine sanctuaries are areas of ocean around coasts, established to protect local wildlife and educate the public about the marine environment. Why not plan a trip to a sanctuary or find out more about them through the Internet? You can also join organizations working to protect and conserve the world's oceans.

Otter in the Monterey Bay National Marine Sanctuary, off the coast of California

Glossary

Bioluminescence

ABYSSAL PLAIN The flat floor of an ocean basin covered in a layer of sediment. (*see also* BASIN, SEDIMENT)

ANTARCTIC Region at the South Pole, south of the Antarctic Circle.

ARCTIC Region at the North Pole, north of the Arctic Circle.

ATOLL Coral reef surrounding a lagoon, growing on the rim of a sunken volcanic island.

BARRIER REEF Coral reef lying parallel to the shore with a wide, deep strip of water between the land and the reef.

BASIN Large, natural bowl-shaped indentation in the Earth's crust. The Atlantic, Pacific, and Indian Oceans lie in three such basins.

BATHYSCAPHE A deep-diving vessel consisting of a spherical cabin suspended beneath a gas-filled float.

BATHYSPHERE Manned, spherical cabin lowered by a cable; the first diving vessel used to study the deep sea.

BIOLUMINESCENCE Meaning living (bio) light (luminescence)—the production of light by a living organism. Some deep-sea creatures produce their own light. In others, it is produced by bacteria living in them.

BIVALVE Soft-bodied animal living in a hinged shell, such as a clam or oyster.

BLACK SMOKER Tall chimneylike vent on the ocean floor that belches out sulfur-rich, super-hot water stained with dark chemicals, used by some deep-sea creatures to make food. Black smokers occur at volcanically active spots on mid-ocean ridges. (see also MID-OCEAN RIDGE)

BONY FISH Fish such as mackerel or cod with a bony skeleton and a swim bladder to control buoyancy.

CARTILAGINOUS FISH Fish such as a shark or ray, with a gristly or cartilaginous skeleton and no swim bladder, meaning it will sink if it doesn't keep moving.

CEPHALOPOD Type of mollusk with a soft body and suckered tentacles, such as a squid.

CONTINENTAL CRUST The Earth's crust that forms the continents.

CONTINENTAL DRIFT Theory that the world's continents were once a single mass of land that slowly drifted apart over millions of years, and are still moving today.

CONTINENTAL SHELF Sloping submerged land at the edge of a continent.

CONTINENTAL SLOPE Sloping submerged land that descends from the continental shelf to the abyssal plain, forming the side of an ocean basin. (*see also* ABYSSAL PLAIN, BASIN)

COPEPOD Tiny shrimplike creature, forming part of the ocean's zooplankton. (*see also* ZOOPLANKTON)

Krill

CRINOID Sea lily that grows on the seabed below 330 ft (100 m); a relative of the feather star.

CRUSTACEAN Animal, such as a lobster or a crab, with jointed legs and a tough, jointed outer skeleton over its body.

CURRENT Body of water that flows through the sea; there are both surface and deep water currents.

DARK ZONE Area of the ocean bordered by the twilight zone above and the abyss below, from around 3,300 and 13,200 ft (1,000 and 4,000 m). Also called the bathypelagic zone. The only light in this zone is from bioluminescent organisms. (see also BIOLUMINESCENCE)

DIATOM Single-celled alga and type of phytoplankton that floats near the ocean's surface, forming the basis of an ocean food chain or food web; common in cool waters.

DINOFLAGELLATE Single-celled alga and a type of phytoplankton, common in warm, tropical waters.

DNA Short for deoxyribonucleic acid—the primary genetic material of a cell that makes up genes and chromosomes.

DORSAL FIN Fin on the back of a fish that helps it keep its balance as it swims.

ECHINODERM Marine invertebrate with spines in the skin, such as a starfish.

EL NINO Warm water current that flows east toward the western coast of South America every few years, causing worldwide weather changes.

FOOD CHAIN Chain or series of plants and animals linked by their feeding relation-ships. A food chain usually includes algae, or plants, plant-eating animals, and meat-eating animals.

FOOD WEB A series of several interlinked food chains.

FRINGING REEF Reef running along a shoreline, with little or no space between the reef and the land.

Swirling winds of a hurricane forming over the Atlantic

Starfish (an echinoderm)

GUYOT Flat-topped seamount that once rose above the ocean's surface as a volcanic island and whose surface was eroded by wind and waves. (*see also* SEAMOUNT)

HURRICANE Tropical storm with winds of over 74 mph (119 km/h), forming over the Atlantic Ocean. Tropical storms are usually called typhoons in the Pacific Ocean and cyclones in the Indian Ocean.

ICEBERG Floating mass of ice broken off an ice sheet or glacier, carried along by ocean currents.

INVERTEBRATE Animal without a backbone.

KRILL Shrimplike crustacean that lives in polar waters of the Arctic and Antarctic in great numbers, forming much of the food supply of baleen whales.

MAGMA Molten rock that lies beneath the Earth's crust.

MARINE BIOLOGY The study of ocean life.

MIDOCEAN RIDGE Long, undersea mountain range forming where two tectonic plates are pulling apart, with magma rising from beneath the Earth's surface and hardening into rock.

MOLLUSK An invertebrate with a soft body usually enclosed by a shell. Mollusks include bivalves (such as clams), gastropods (such as sea slugs), and cephalopods (such as squid and octopuses). (*see also* BIVALVE, CEPHALOPOD)

OCEANOGRAPHY The scientific study of the oceans.

PHYTOPLANKTON Microscopic single-celled algae that drift in the ocean's sunlit zone. (*see also* SUNLIT ZONE)

PLANKTON Tiny plant and animal organisms that drift in the sea's surface waters, providing the basis of most marine food chains. (*see also* FOOD CHAIN, ZOOPLANKTON)

PLATE TECTONICS The study of the movement of the Earth's lithospheric plates that carry the oceanic and continental crust.

POLYP A sea anemone or coral with a mouth surrounded by tentacles. A hard coral polyp makes a limestone cup, or skeleton, to protect its body. Thousands of polyps live together in colonies, forming a coral reef.

ROV Short for Remotely Operated Vehicle— a small vessel operated from (and tethered to) a submersible or ship.

SALINITY The amount of dissolved salt in seawater. Salinity is measured as parts of salt per 1,000 parts of seawater, the average salinity of the oceans being 35 parts of salt per 1,000 parts of seawater.

SCUBA Stands for Self-Contained Underwater Breathing Apparatus—SCUBA divers carry their own air supply in tanks on their backs.

SEA Another word for ocean, or a particular part of an ocean—for example, the Black Sea and the Mediterranean Sea are connected to the Atlantic Ocean.

SEAMOUNT Underwater volcano that rises 3,300 ft (1,000 m) or more above the surrounding plain.

SEDIMENT Mud, sand, and silt, containing millions of tiny plants and animals, washed off the land by rivers. Sediment settles on the ocean floor.

SONAR Short for Sound Navigation And Ranging—a system that can locate the position of an object by emitting sounds then timing the echoes that bounce back.

SUBMERSIBLE Manned or remotely operated underwater research submarine designed to withstand water pressure in deep water. (*see also* WATER PRESSURE)

SUNLIT ZONE Surface layer of the ocean penetrated by sunlight, to around 650 ft (200 m) deep. Most marine life lives in this zone. Also called the epipelagic zone.

SYMBIOSIS Close interaction between two different species where either, both, or neither benefit from the relationship.

TIDE The regular rise and fall of the sea caused by the gravitational pull of the Sun and the Moon on the Earth.

TRENCH A steep-sided trough or valley in the ocean floor.

TSUNAMI Sea wave usually caused by an underwater volcanic eruption or earthquake. It can cause great damage if it reaches the coast as it may gain considerable height in shallow water. Sometimes wrongly called a tidal wave.

Black smoker

Submersible

TWILIGHT ZONE Area of the ocean from around 650–3,300 ft (200–1,000 m) deep, bordered by the sunlit zone above and darkness below. Also called the mesopelagic zone.

TYPHOON Name given to a tropical storm in the western Pacific Ocean. (*see also* HURRICANE)

UPWELLING Rising of nutrient–rich water from deeper parts of the ocean to the surface.

WATER PRESSURE Force exerted by water because of its weight and density; water pressure increases by one atmosphere for each 33 ft (10 m) depth.

WAVE HEIGHT The distance between the crest (top of a wave) and its trough (lowest part of a wave).

WAVELENGTH The vertical distance between two successive wave crests (the tops of the waves).

ZOOPLANKTON Tiny animals that float in the water, such as copepods and tiny crustaceans, forming part of plankton. (*see also* PHYTOPLANKTON, PLANKTON)

Index

Acknowledgments

The publisher would like to thank:
for their invaluable assistance during photography: The University Marine Biological Station, Scotland, especially Prof. Johon Davenport, David Murden, Bobbie Wilkie, Donald Patrick, Phil Lonsdale, Ken Cameron, Dr. Jason Hall-Spencer, Simon Thurston, Steve Parker, Geordie Campbell, and Helen Thirlwall; Sea Life Centres (UK), especially Robin James, David Copp, Patrick van der Menve, and Ian Shaw (Weymouth); and Marcus Goodsir (Portsmouth); Colin Pelton, Peter Hunter, Dr. Brian Bett, and Mike Conquer of the Institute of Oceanographic Sciences;Tim Parmenter, Simon Caslaw, and Paul Ruddock of the Natural History Museum, London; Margaret Bidmead of the Royal Navy Submarine Museum, Gosport; IFREMER for their kind permission to photograph the model of Nautile; David Fowler of Deep Sea Adventure. Mak Graham, Andrew and Richard Pierson of Otterferry Salmon Ltd; Bob Donalson of Angus Modelmakers; Sally Rose for additional research; Kathy Lockley for providing

props; Helena Spiteri, Djinn von Noorden, Susan St. Louis, Ivan Finnegan, joe Hoyle, Mark Haygarth, and David Pickering for editorial and design assistance; Stewart J. Wild for proof-reading; David Ekholm–JAlbum, Sunita Gahir, Susan St. Louis, Carey Scott, Lisa Stock, and Bulent Yusuf for the clip art; Neville Graham, Sue Nicholson, and Susan St. Louis for the wall chart; Margaret Parrish and Christine Heilman for Americanization.

The publishers would also like to thank Trevor Day for his assistance on the paperback edition.

Picture credits:
The publisher would like to thank the following for their kind permission to reproduce their photographs:
a=above, b=below, c=center, l=left, r=right, t=top

Alamy Images: Paul Glendell 60tr; **American Museum of Natural History:** 11tl (no. 419(2)); **Heather Angel** 38bc; **Ardea**/Val Taylor 62 cr;

Tracy Bowden/Pedro Borrell: 55 tc. **Bridgeman Art Library**/Prado, Madrid 9tr; Uffizi Gallery, Florence 16tr: **Bruce Coleman Ltd**/Carl Roessler 22c;Frieder Sauer 26tr; Charles & Sandra Hood 27tc; Jeff Foott 28tr, 56tr; Jane Burton 38bl; Michael Roggo 57tr Orion service & Trading Co. 58br; Atlantide SDF 59tr; Nancy Selton 63br; to Library: 7br; **Steven J. Cooling** 60br. **Corbis:** Jerome Sessini 60–61b; Ralph White 67c. 71bc; Roger Wood 67tr; Tom Stewart 66br. **The Deep,** Hull: Craig Stennet/Guzelian 68cr. **Mary Evans Picture Library** 11tr, 12tr, 19tl, 20tl, 28tl, 33tr, 34tr, 40cl. 45tr, 48tr, 49tl, 50bl, 52tr. 54c. **Getty Images:** Nikolas Konstatinou 69tl, Will & Den McIntype 66bl. **Ronald Grant Archive** 42cl, 55bl. **Robert Harding Picture Library** 25tl, 32tr, 32bc, 39br, 57tr, 63tl. **Institute of Oceanographic Sciences:** 46lc. **Jamstec:** 66cl. © Japanese Meteorological Agency/Meteorological Office 12l. **Frank Lane Photo Agency**/M. Neqwman 11br; **Simon Conway Moiris:** 6tr. **N.H.P.A.**/ Agence natur 44c, Linda and Brian Pitkin 67tl; Peter Parks 64bl. **National Oceanography Centre, Southampton:** 53br. **Nature Picture Library:** David Shale 70tl: Doc White 65b; Fabio Liverani 65tr; Ieff Foott 69cl; Jurgen Freund 64–65; Peter Scoones 65cl; Thomas D. Mangelsen 69b. **Oxford Scientific Films**/toi de Roy 29t;

Fred Bavendam 43 tl; David Cayless 68bl, 68-69; Howard Hall 64tr; Rick Price/SAL 67b; Scott Winer 70-71. **Planet Earth Pictures**/Peter Scoones 9tl; Norbert Wu 10-11c, 20cl, 40tr, 40tl, 4lt, 42tr; Gary Bell 23br, 55tr; Mark Conlin 25c, 36br; Menuhin 29tc; Ken Lucas 30tl; NevilJe Coleman 33cr; Steve Bloom 37c; Andrew Mounter 38br; Larry Madin 43 br; Ken Vaughari 51 cr; Georgette Doowma 63cr. **Science Photo Library**/Dr. G. Feldman 26bl: Ron Church 53 cr; Douglas Faulkner 66cr; Simon Fraser 62bl; NASA/Goddard Space Flight Centre 70br; Tom Van Sant, Geosphere Project/Planetary, Visions 64cl. **Frank Spooner Pictures:** 47t, 47cr, 54br, 54bl, 60bl, 61t. **Tony Stone Images:** Jeff Rotman 53lc. **Stoll Comex Seaway Ltd:** 61tl. **Town Cocks Museum,** Hull 63tr. **ZEFA:** 36cl,56ct.

Wall chart credits: Corbis: Gary Bell / zefa cl (shoal); Martin Harvey / Gallo Images br (oil spill)

Jacket credits: *Front:* Corbis: Tim Davis c.
Back: DK Images: Courtesy of IFREMER, Paris cra.

All other images © Dorling Kindersley.
For further information see:
www.dkimages.com